COUNTERSTORIES FROM
THE WRITING CENTER

T0290719

COUNTERSTORIES FROM THE WRITING CENTER

EDITED BY
WONDERFUL FAISON
AND FRANKIE CONDON

UTAH STATE UNIVERSITY PRESS
Logan

© 2022 by University Press of Colorado

Published by Utah State University Press
An imprint of University Press of Colorado
245 Century Circle, Suite 202
Louisville, Colorado 80027

 The University Press of Colorado is a proud member of
the Association of University Presses.

The University Press of Colorado is a cooperative publishing enterprise supported,
in part, by Adams State University, Colorado State University, Fort Lewis College,
Metropolitan State University of Denver, Regis University, University of Alaska Fairbanks,
University of Colorado, University of Northern Colorado, University of Wyoming, Utah
State University, and Western Colorado University.

ISBN: 978-1-64642-152-7 (paperback)
ISBN: 978-1-64642-153-4 (ebook)
https://doi.org/10.7330/9781646421534

Library of Congress Cataloging-in-Publication Data

Names: Faison, Wonderful, editor. | Condon, Frankie, editor.
Title: CounterStories from the writing center / edited by Wonderful Faison and Frankie Condon.
Description: Logan : Utah State University Press, [2021] | Includes bibliographical references and index.
Identifiers: LCCN 2021029478 (print) | LCCN 2021029479 (ebook) | ISBN 9781646421527 (paperback) | ISBN 9781646421534 (epub)
Subjects: LCSH: Writing centers—Administration. | Racism in higher education. | English language—Rhetoric—Study and teaching (Higher) | English teachers—Training of.
Classification: LCC PE1404 .C639 2021 (print) | LCC PE1404 (ebook) | DDC 808/.042071173—dc23
LC record available at https://lccn.loc.gov/2021029478
LC ebook record available at https://lccn.loc.gov/2021029479

Cover illustration © agsandrew/Shutterstock.

To daddy—and to my mama who is lost. We will find you.
~Wonderful Faison

For Dan, Lucy, and Grace
~Frankie Condon

CONTENTS

SECTION THREE: ESSAYING WHITE ANTI-RACISM

    the Writing Center
    Nicole I. Caswell   109

9. A Long Path to *Semi*-Woke
    Jill Reglin   120

10. Stories of Activist Allies in the Writing Center
    Dianna Baldwin and Trixie G. Smith   133

    Afterword
    Neisha-Anne S. Green and Frankie Condon   145

    Index   161
    About the Authors   163

FOREWORD

Aja Y. Martinez

"Knock knock, good morning Alejandra!"

Slightly startled out of her thoughts, Alejandra Prieto looked up from her laptop to find the friendly face of Aaliyah, the writing center's student worker, peeking around the cubicle wall.

"Morning, Aaliyah," Alejandra replied with a smile. "Is my 11 am here?"

"Yup," said Aaliyah with an affirmative nod, "want me to send her back?"

"Sure, I'm ready," Alejandra said, closing her laptop and clearing the scatter of articles that had spread across the small consulting table.

Listening for the approaching footsteps of her 11 am appointment, Alejandra gazed out the floor-to-ceiling window that served as a third wall of sorts to her small cubicle. As she watched students and staff hurriedly walk in various directions, and feeling ever like a fish in a fishbowl, Alejandra wondered about these giant windows. Did they intend to communicate a certain transparency to the inner workings and goings on of the Writing Center (WC)? And, did this third wall represent a sort of invitational gesture to would-be consultees?

"Hello, Miss Alejandra," said an accented voice from outside her thoughts.

Quickly switching her gaze from the window to the cubicle opening, Alejandra saw a delicate-featured and bronze-skinned Asian woman standing uncertainly at her table.

"Oh hello . . .," Alejandra said, scanning the paperwork she was handed for her name.

"Melati," the woman offered, filling Alejandra's pause with a name.

"Thanks," Alejandra replied congenially, "welcome, Melati, why don't you take a seat," she said, gesturing to the seat next to hers.

https://doi.org/10.7330/9781646421534.c000a

Melati remained standing, still looking uncertain, and then said, "What I would like to know first is, what *is* this 'Writing Center'? And *why* has my professor sent me here *before* we've even written anything in his course?"

Not expecting these questions, Alejandra took a few moments to consider a response, once again taking in Melati's Brown skin, her Asian features, and her accented English. Considering their context at this predominantly and historically white and private university, Alejandra could wager a guess or two as to *why* Melati's professor sent her to the campus WC.

Still thinking about Melati's appointment during her traffic-ridden drive home that evening, Alejandra called the only person she could think of to help her untangle her thoughts—her friend from grad school, Jessica Columbo. Jessica, a WC administrator and theorist in her own right, had crafted and collaborated on plenty of scholarship that helped Alejandra think through her positionality as a consultant (Cirillo-McCarthy 2014; Cirillo-McCarthy et al. 2016), so Alejandra thought it only fitting to call her good friend for some advice.

After a few minutes of general hellos and catching up, Alejandra got to the point. Because her first opportunity to *work* in a writing center as a consultant didn't occur until she was in the second job of her career, well into her career as a tenure-track professor, Alejandra was very much now living the reality that had been so well recounted, studied, and theorized in field-specific conversations and existing literatures (Villanueva 2006; Geller et al. 2007; Greenfield and Rowan 2011; McKinney 2013).

"What was most troubling," Alejandra continued, "is that this student, Melati, had no idea *why* she had been sent to the WC. And I understand her confusion. It's only week two in the semester, they've not yet written anything substantial beyond blog responses in this course, and according to Melati, her professor just referred her to the center without contextualizing what we do."

Hearing Jessica's "tutting" click of tongue against teeth, Alejandra could imagine her friend shaking her head in dismay.

"What program and class are Melati enrolled in?" Jessica asked.

"She's here to get her MBA, so the class is some sort of 'Writing for Business' course offered by the School of Management—and get this!" Alejandra continued, "She's from Indonesia and already has a law degree—she told me she's a pretty prominent real estate attorney in Jakarta!"

"Wow." Jessica exhaled, sounding exasperated.

"I guess my frustration is that I *know*, I mean, I've read and listened to the conversations in our field by WC folks about these sorts of situations occurring—situations where professors seemingly just preemptively push students off to the WC after making assumptions about their writing and language abilities—"

"Yes, too often racist or xenophobic assumptions," Jessica interjected.

"Exactly," Alejandra affirmed. "I mean, what other reason at this point in the semester could have prompted this professor to just send Melati to us without an assignment to work on?"

"So how did you spend the consulting time?" Jessica prompted.

"Well, I began by giving her a run-down of the sorts of services we offer to support students with written assignments, and out of curiosity, I asked to see Melati's couple blog responses that she had written for this course."

"And let me guess, her writing is fine?"

"Yes!" Alejandra exclaimed. "Aside from a few inconsistencies with articles and prepositions, her writing is fine. And yeah, she speaks English with an accent, she's a person of color, and she's international—but she already has an advanced degree and is here in this prestigious and competitive school of management seeking a second advanced degree. I mean, what was this professor thinking sending her to us before they've even really started, before he's really even had time to assess her writing?"

"He's likely thinking about himself," Jessica stated simply. Continuing, she said, "But he has probably also convinced himself that he's actually just looking out for her—it's a classic case of good ol' colonial benevolence."

"And ignorance too," I added. "Melati and I ended up spending the majority of the appointment talking about English-language imperialism, and the ways in which it's a linguistic supremacy here in the U.S."

"Mmmhmm," Jessica agreed.

"And what really gets me, is that I can't help but wonder if this professor has any proficiency—spoken or written—in any languages other than SAE (Standard American English)?"

"Probably not," Jessica responded. "Here in the states it's not like it's a requirement of the profession to know anything other than English—there's that 'proficiency requirement' that some grad programs still have, but even those are beginning to get phased out—"

"Right! Exactly!" Alejandra replied, "And even those proficiency hoops they set up in grad school don't always get it right. Take my case for example: I was raised in the U.S./Mexico borderlands, so I definitely have linguistic proficiency in borderlands English AND Spanish, but emphasis on the *borderlands* variety, because as you well know, this is not the version these 'proficiency' exams test for" (Martinez 2016).

"Nope," Jessica confirmed. "It's the Castilian form, and I remember well when they made you take that semester-long Spanish grammar course when we were in grad school—all because your translation of that paragraph from English to Spanish wasn't the version of Spanish the institution would sanction as 'demonstrating proficiency.'"

"Yep, and all you *gringas* in my cohort passed it with flying colors!" Alejandra said in an annoyed tone but adding a playful laugh.

"Yet you were the only one of our group who could actually communicate effectively with the community and in the barrios—you were the only one of our cohort actually *of* the community, how is that not a second language 'proficiency'?!"

"Yeah, I know," Alejandra replied, "and these sort of lived realities and experiences are where the conversation with Melati led. Her lived reality is that she's fluent in four languages! She told me she can read and write in three of those languages, and that she writes at the academic level in two of them! How many U.S. born and raised professors at my institution—or really any U.S. institution—can say that?"

"I'm sure too few to even account for any sort of statistical representation," Jessica surmised.

"Right. So that's what got my cogs really turning—this whole idea of experiences, and the narratives that accompany those experiences, and the ways the lack of awareness of these lived realities of our students lends itself to a benevolence devoid of empathy on the part of some teachers."

"You know, that's spot on," Jessica began, "because my guess is that if professors like the one Melati is dealing with had any semblance of experience with what it's like to attempt just *spoken* proficiency with a language outside their first language—well geez! They'd at least appreciate how *hard* grammar really is!"

"Exactly! And then add the incredibly difficult dimension of not just speaking with proficiency, but also writing with proficiency—in SAE academese no less!" Alejandra said.

"And lacking an awareness of Melati's story, combined with a personal lacking in lived experience with linguistic juggling—well, now the picture of this professor forms up pretty clearly—and how representative is this picture of professors in relation to students of color and/or/also international students at our institutions? If only these students' stories were known," Jessica said, wistfully.

"But I have to point out that it's *not* the responsibility of the student to educate the teacher about these lived realities."

"Right," Jessica affirmed, "it really should be the teacher who seeks out this sort of knowledge as part of their own professionalization, as part of honing their skill and craft as an educator who will undoubtedly interact with students from different backgrounds, foreign countries, and varying linguistic situations. And in an effort *not* to make assumptions and *not* to do harm to students based on things like race, class, national origin, or language, educators really need to take the time to engage students' narratives and experiences. These lived realities should serve as a foundation to an educator's flexible and ever-evolving praxis."

"I completely agree," Alejandra replied. "In fact, I've had recent opportunity to read an advance copy of a forthcoming manuscript about exactly this topic that I think will be essential reading for teachers and WC administrators and consultants."

"Oh yeah?" said Jessica with interest. "What's it called?"

"*CounterStories from the Writing Center*, edited by Wonderful Faison and Frankie Condon."

"I can't wait to read it," Jessica said.

COUNTERSTORIES FROM THE WRITING CENTER

INTRODUCTION

Wonderful Faison and Frankie Condon

We met by happenstance one afternoon in a bar in Portland, Oregon. Both of us were attending the Conference on College Composition and Communication and Frankie was having a drink and heart-to-heart conversation with one of the authors in this collection. Wonderful was sitting at the next table. Of our meeting, Wonderful writes,

> I remember you discussing something that had to do with racism in the academy and in the writing center and my ears perked. I will be honest: I didn't know who you or Romeo were. I just wanted to know, as I sat at the table drinking my whiskey, who these thoughtful people were talking so eloquently and so truthfully about the university, the writing center, and how the writing center reproduces systemic injustice, and more specifi- cally, systemic racism. I had to chime in, give my two cents, drop the mic if you will I introduced myself, "Hi, I'm Wonderful. Sorry to interrupt. Y'all just said some things that spoke to my heart and I had to say somethin bout that." You, very graciously, said, "I know you. I've heard of you," to which I could only reply, "Oh God, what lies have people been tellin you about me?" We exchanged numbers and over the course of mentorship, conversation, and you providing feedback on articles I intended to pub- lish, we formed a bond of both friendship and scholarship. We wanted to write together and speak truth to power. And so, the journey to this book began, but the journey of our friendship began at that restaurant with me as an eavesdropper, listening, waiting, praying for a moment to jump in and say something to the fair faced [presumed white] woman who actually seemed to be LISTENING to a Brown man. There is comfort, my friend, in those who listen, value, and are active participants in change. There is comfort, my friend, in you.

In the years since our first meeting, we have talked by telephone fre- quently and texted—often daily—slowly and tenderly forming a bond of friendship, camaraderie, and alliance. We have shared our writing with one another, but also shared the everyday joys and struggles of our lives in the academy and beyond. In some sense, we have defied those historical conditions that agitate against sustained friendship—against trust—between women of colour and white women. We have learned again and anew how powerfully those conditions wind through our

https://doi.org/10.7330/9781646421534.c000b

relations such that the crafting of such a friendship and of the care, compassion, and loyalty that compose it must always be an ongoing process. We must learn from one another, about one another, and for one another even as we acknowledge and resist the ways and degrees to which racism and white supremacy insert themselves between us. Of such friendships, Frankie writes,

> As we began to correspond with one another after the day we met, you were bold—in the best sense. You asked me to read and respond to your work. You asked me good, hard questions about why I think the way I do and do the work I try to do. You called me into—continue to call me into—a critical self-reflection that is not self-serving so much as it is necessary to the creation of enduring friendship. As we have talked and written to one another, I, too, have leaned on you—asking your advice, running ideas past you, trusting your judgement when mine seems inadequate to some occasion or other. There is, I mean to say, reciprocity between us; we are learning to need one another not in any burdensome sense, but as friends and, as Neisha-Anne Green would say, as accomplices in the labour for social justice that each of us can do from where we stand in the world and in our fields.

Years ago, Dr. Vershawn Young and Frankie were leading an anti-racism workshop at a university in the Midwest. They had asked the participants to get into small groups to address a query. One of the groups was composed of four young white women. After some time, one of them beckoned to Frankie to join them. There was some hemming and hawing and then, finally, one of the group members asked her, "Dr. Condon, what did you do to make Dr. Vay want to be friends with you?" She smiled at the question. After the workshop, Frankie told Dr. Vay what the group had asked—and laughed at the memory. Responding to her laughter, Dr. Vay said, "but that's a really good question to be asking and for you to be answering." Frankie has forgotten exactly what she said in response to the women who asked. But she thinks she said that she tries to tell the truth about racism and white supremacy as best she can discern it from where she stands. Not to affirm that truth as all that needs to be known but rather to recognize both her ability to see and what she fails to see as already interwoven with the lived experience of racism, white supremacy, and white privilege that conditions and constrains the lives of peoples of colour. She says she probably wasn't that eloquent, though, as she was, she admits, surprised and taken aback by the question.

In some sense, the collection we offer to you here is driven by what we imagine was the animating sense of both need and desire beneath the question posed to Frankie on that day. What, we continue to wonder, are the necessary conditions—the shifts in consciousness, commitment, understanding, and care required of raced-white peoples working in writing centres today—cis-gendered, trans, heterosexual, queer, all—if they are to act, really act, as the accomplices of peoples of colour in the struggle for social justice from within and beyond their institutional sites? This book, however, is predicated particularly on our collective recognition of the dominant role white, straight, cis-gendered women (SCG) have played in writing centre administration as well as in the field of writing centre studies. Our concern is not with individual white women in writing centres but with the social, political, and cultural capital that is the historical birthright of white SCG women, generally, in nations (Canada and the United States) "stamped from the beginning" by white supremacy as well as by racism (Kendi). Our concern—and the concern of the writers whose work is collected in this volume—is the ways in which this legacy has been made manifest in writing centre scholarship, practice, tutor education, and writing centre design and management. And we are most particularly concerned with the lived experiences of tutors, scholars, and directors of colour in writing centre spaces that are also stamped from the beginning.

The essays collected in this volume test, defy, and often overflow the bounds of traditional academic discourse. This is not accidental—not a matter of mistakes made by writers—but rather a purposeful, political choice. Corder (1995) writes, in his pivotal essay, "Argument as Emergence, Rhetoric as Love," that we are all narrators making sense of our lives and of our relations through the stories we tell. Corder notes that our narratives often fit seamlessly with one another or we order our lives in order that we may spend them with those whose stories neither trouble nor challenge our own. But sometimes, he writes, we encounter stories that so destabilize the meanings we have narrated for our own lives that we struggle to account for them. In such cases, Corder argues, we may refuse to hear these othered, these *counter*stories; sometimes, he says, we go to war with one another in order to silence them; sometimes they drive us to madness. But sometimes, Corder suggests, we may choose to listen, may yield to the trouble, the challenge, and allow ourselves to be changed, our narratives to be transformed in the yielding.

Wonderful writes:

> But what all can a book do? White people love books so much, as if they provide some divine knowledge or knowledges they lack. I find, white people do know about racism and white supremacy and yet, they do not care. I find white people refuse to listen, to hear, and thus are willfully ignorant of the fact of racism in all of our lives. People of Color have said

this before. People of Color have rung the bell many times about the injustices both within and outside the academy and yet, we are asked repeatedly to reproduce, to regurgitate the words of my academic ancestors and answer "how does racism, sexism, classism, homophobia, etc. exist in the academy?" And that reproduction, that regurgitation, that vomiting up of what white folks have refused to hear again and again is considered new and transcendent—for about five minutes . . . till they forget again. This is not knowledge and the message is not new. This is the same beating of the same drum. This is the same broken record, scratched cd, the Pandora song that cannot be skipped. Scholars of color could be extraordinary contributors to the field of writing center studies, no doubt, if only we were not asked to repeat ourselves over and over again. And writing center scholarship and practice might actually change if only we focused less on pushing the field forward and more on pushing ourselves, our writing centers, our people, and our society in uncompromising and uncomfortable ways towards justice, truth, and yes, freedom.

In his study of colourblind racism, *Racism without Racists: Color-Blind Racism & the Persistence of Racial Inequality in Contemporary America*, sociologist Eduardo Bonilla-Silva (2003) notes that "storytelling often represents the most ideological moments" (p. 75). Frequently, Bonilla-Silva writes, we craft our stories, narrate our lives as if "there was *only one way* of telling them" and as if understanding them were a matter of common sense (p. 75). We narrate our lives, in other words, absent awareness of the ways our stories are ideologically infused and, for the purposes of this book, saturated with dominant racial ideology. Bonilla-Silva writes that "ideologies are about 'meaning in the service of power.' They are expressions at the symbolic level of the fact of dominance" (p. 25). "The ideologies of the powerful," he notes, "are central in the production and reinforcement of the status quo" (pp. 25–26). Bonilla-Silva (2003) argues further that racial ideology provides us with particular frames that are its "set paths for interpreting information" as well as with a particular style (p. 26). "The style of an ideology," he writes, "refers to its peculiar *linguistic manners and rhetorical strategies (or race talk)*" (p. 53). Race talk, Bonilla Silva suggests, enables narrators to craft the connective tissue between "frames and storylines" that compose the racialized stories we tell, however unconsciously and however much we have learned to tell and interpret them as common sense (p. 53).

Thus, critical race theorists have long theorized the significance of counter-narrative—of counterstory—to the project of intervening, interrogating, and disrupting the rules of racial standing under white supremacy. Critical race theorists have recognized the conjoinment of racial order (the rules of racial standing), race talk, and even the most implicit practices of white supremacy and racism within predominantly white institutions and the systems of which they are a part (the legal system, for example, and the criminal justice system) (Bell 1992, Williams 1992, Delgado 1989, for example). Counterstory, they argue, performs a kind of double-duty. First, counterstory exposes the everyday erasures, exclusions, and repression of narratives of People of Colour's lived experience—narratives that trouble, challenge, and destabilize "meaning in the service of power," its frames, its style, or rhetoric. Second, counterstory enables the interrogation and disruption of the everyday practice of racism and white supremacy. Counterstory insists on the legibility and intelligibility of that which has been treated as illegible and unintelligible under the aegis of white supremacist discourse: the racial Other, her lived experience, her resistance, refusal, survival, her brilliance—and the languages, discourses, genres in which she speaks her being. In his book *Faces at the Bottom of the Well: The Permanence of Racism*, Derrick Bell (1992) notes that counterstory affirms and uplifts Peoples of Colour as they hear the truth of their lived experience under racism named. But Bell argues also that the creative truth-telling that constitutes counterstory is, in fact, designed to "harass" white people: to unsettle the commonplace nature of racism and white supremacy that sustains both their comfort and their privilege.

In the field of writing studies, Aja Martinez's work on counterstory deeply informs our understanding of the significance of the genre to the work of anti-racism in writing centre contexts. In the first chapter of her book, *Counterstory: The Rhetoric and Writing of Critical Race Theory*, Martinez (2020) traces the genealogy of critical race theory (CRT) and the relationship of counterstory to that discipline. "Counterstory," writes Martinez, "is both method and methodology—it is a method for telling stories of those people whose experiences are not often told, and, as informed by CRT, this methodology serves to expose, analyze, and challenge majoritarian stories of racialized privilege and can help to strengthen traditions of social, political, and cultural survival, resistance, and justice" (p. 26). Connecting both CRT and counterstory to the field of writing studies, Martinez (2020) writes, "CRT provides scholars in rhetoric and writing studies . . . an ability to bring to the foreground the workings of racism in the daily lives of all people, and it further illustrates that we all function within the hegemony of systems of domination and subordination, advantage and disadvantage, structured according to racial categories" (p. 27). Martinez argues that writing studies scholars and teachers—and, we think, by extension, writing centre scholars and practitioners—have a moral and political as well as pedagogical responsibility to contend with and resist theories and methods in our field(s) "that dismiss or decenter racism, and those whose lives are daily affected by it" (p. 26). Martinez (2020) clarifies for those who are new to counterstory, that "counterstory as methodology is the verb, the process, the critical race theory–informed justification for the work (Delgado Bernal et al. 364); whereas counterstory as method is the noun, the genre, the research tool" (p. 2). We take as a grounding principle for this book that CRT (critical race theory) and counterstory are powerful means of surfacing, naming, interrogating, and dismantling the workings of racism in the daily life of the writing centre.

Drawing together the threads of narrative and discourse theory from the fields of rhetoric, sociology, and critical race theory, this book is anchored in our collective critique of the continued domination of writing centre studies and its undergirding racial narratives by white, straight, cis-gendered women—whether or not, as individuals, they/we *intend* by our scholarship or pedagogical practice to reproduce a racial status quo. We believe that dominant writing centre theory continues to be cast in *whitely* discourse (frames and style, as Bonilla-Silva employs the term) and thus continues to promote one-with-one pedagogies that are both animated by *whiteliness* and promote *whiteliness* as the enabling condition for academic discourse. Drawing on Frye and, following from Frye, Condon's theorization of the term, we understand whiteliness as an epistemological cum rhetorical positioning that advances the position of speakers possessing the social capital and power accrued under conditions of white supremacy. The whitely speaker is the arbiter of value who may justifiably enact "a staggering faith in their own rightness and goodness," as well as in the rightness and goodness of those social interests their adjudication, martyrdom, and ministry represent, insisting that they will not be moved and the interests they represent will not be changed unless and until "the moves [toward change] are made in appropriate ways" (Frye, 1992, pp. 90–91; Condon, 2017, pp. 34–36). We understand that whiteliness is not associated necessarily with the race with which any speaker may identify. The writers in this volume recognize, however, the particular position of empowerment many raced-white women have held in the field of writing centre studies—both as scholars of note and as ranking administrators.

Pursuing Condon's application of the term "whiteliness" to the teaching and tutoring of writing, we argue that despite the important contributions of prior writing center scholarship to the field's understanding and address of social justice, equality, and equity, generally speaking, the field's shared sense of best practices for the tutoring of writing continues to be underwritten by implicit and explicit beliefs associated with a particularly raced and gendered (WSCG) benevolence or *noblesse oblige* (2018; 2019). Thus, the writing centre participates in the institutionalized practice of cannibalizing the cultures and languages of Othered bodies; enforcing the assimilation of student writers and tutors of color into whitely discourses and the epistemological spaces in which those discourses are legitimated and reproduced. Whitely writing centres, we think, participate in the academy's racial project of defining and containing racial Otherness within acceptable, normative limits, thus preserving white advantage and privilege.

To be clear, we are particularly admiring of recent writing center scholarship that contends with inequities in the writing center that are the effects of racism, sexism, homophobia, transphobia, ableism, and ethnocentrism, especially *Out in the Center: Public Controversies and Private Struggles*, a book addressing identity matters in the writing center from an intersectional standpoint that embraces narrative not as distinct from theorization but integral to the knowledge-making endeavor. We admire Greenfield's recent book, *Radical Writing Center Praxis: A Paradigm for Ethical Political Engagement*, not only for what she says but also for the wellsprings of hope her work taps. This book, however, concerns itself with the ways and degrees to which, despite this growing focus by writing center scholars on social justice matters, writing centers, in the main and on the ground, remain institutional sites dedicated to assimilationism and the preservation and reproduction of a status quo within and beyond the academy that privileges not merely whiteness, but idealized white, straight, cis-gendered womanhood as well. *CounterStories from the Writing Center* is not intended as a tutoring guide (although we believe tutors should read it). Nor is *CounterStories* intended to teach writing centre directors how to manage anti-racist writing centres (although we believe our book will help directors discern how to begin and sustain that work). Instead, *CounterStories* demands that tutors, directors, and scholars step back from that whitely impulse to take charge in fixing all the things. We ask that tutors, directors, and writers first listen and choose to be touched, changed even, by the stories of those whose working lives in writing centres have been conditioned by their lived experience of racism. Only then, we believe, can acknowledgement, address, or redress reasonably be attempted. In service of aiding WSCG readers in learning to recognize and resist their own internalized white supremacy and its attending discourse, whiteliness, *CounterStories* includes both co- and single-authored essays by a diverse group of white women narrating in a variety of ways and at a variety of stages their own attempts to contend with race and racism within and beyond the writing centre. *CounterStories* is predicated on our collective conviction that if multiracial affiliative relations, accomplice relations are possible—if there is to be friendship, camaraderie, across racial lines as we live and work together in our writing centres, all of us have some hard work to do.

CounterStories is edgy and we have not attempted to smooth or disguise its edges. Its authors tell stories that hurt to hear and tell them without so much mediation of feeling as is common in more traditional academic texts. They/we are annoyed, frustrated, sad, cynical, enraged as we seek to make visible, articulable, and powerful the lived experiences and living knowledges of those who have been made liminal or constrained within liminality by both explicit and implicit racial orders within the field as well as in the institutions in which we labour. We know that despite a general distrust of conflict, writing centre folks will have to contend with the righteous anger of peoples of colour produced by years of failure on the part of predominantly white systems, institutions, and raced-white peoples to claim and make actionable their commitments to racial justice by dismantling not only the outward signs, but also and more important, the foundations of white supremacy and racism that unequally and unfairly distribute political, social, and economic advantage along racial lines.

And so, we think that readers of this collection should take offense—not at the ways they are called out by the writers whose work they will encounter here, but at the continuing necessity for such books in our field. When readers feel most inclined to put this book down, to refuse it, we hope they will hear also the ways in which its authors call them in, continuing to hope even as we engage with the evidence that racism is real in the places where we work. If, as a field, we are to move, finally, away from the ongoing cycle of hand-wringing, searching out a person of colour for comfort and advice, finding reasons to ignore the witness of scholars, tutors, and writers of colour, then continuing on in the same old way, all of us, but white, straight, cis-gendered women, in particular, will need to yield to the necessity for both humility and courage that is the enabling condition for changing ourselves, our teaching practices, and our world. We will need to stay for and be moved by the righteous anger of peoples of colour. And beyond *feeling* moved, we will need to *move* ourselves—to get on board or get out of the way.

AN INTRODUCTION TO THE CHAPTERS

CounterStories is organized into three sections. Section One, "Calling Out/Calling In," situates the collection as a whole by offering in three variations narrative accounts and critical interventions in white supremacy and whiteliness as they are enacted in the field of writing centre studies as well as in our writing centres. Each of the three essays in Section One both calls readers out and calls them in, insisting that readers attend and also modeling ways of listening, ways of responding, and ways of engaging critically with/against the whitely self.

Section One begins with Green's chapter, "Prophetic Anti-Racist Activism: 'Black Prophetic Fire' REIGNITED." Green calls readers in as she narrates her dissatisfaction with the term—and the idea—of allyship. Offering as an alternative the idea of accompliceship, Green gives voice both to the pain of being a woman of colour in the predominantly, overwhelmingly white field of writing centre studies and to her determination to be an advocate and an agent for change within and beyond the field. Shifting her focus as she speaks alternately to white readers and to readers of colour, Green reminds us of the importance of the work of anti-racism: that lives are at stake and so is our humanity.

In chapter 2, Condon explores the policing of the raced/gendered performances of white women that, she argues, contributes powerfully to the field's inertia—its failures and its systematic slowness to change even as it accommodates and appropriates calls for change. She acknowledges and gives voice to the anger she feels (has long felt) not only at the field but also and perhaps more so at herself for the ways in which she (and the field) are implicated in whiteness.

In chapter 3, "Beyond the Binary: Revealing a Continuum of Racism in Writing Center Theory and Practice," Haltiwanger-Morrison discusses the burgeoning advocacy for anti-racist pedagogy and practice in writing center studies. She notes, however, that even as the field writ large continues to be dominated by the work of white women, so too does the preponderance of this advocacy. Haltiwanger-Morrison argues that white women working in writing centers—even those who often consider themselves allies—regularly enact racism both directly and indirectly. As she explores the lack of racial awareness among WSCG women writing centre directors, Haltiwanger-Morrison narrates her experience of racism in the world of writing centres. Ultimately, she urges writing center scholars to shift their conceptions and perceptions of racism and its enactments from a binary racist/non-racist, to a continuum in service of a more sustained, enduring individual and collective commitment to anti-racism.

Chapter 4, co-authored by Treviño and Ozias, takes up threads introduced in prior chapters, deepening and extending them. Treviño invites both readers of colour and white readers to "move in and out of identifying or disidentifying" with her as she narrates her own coming of age story and, in particular, her conflicted relationship to school. Treviño also reflects on her story, on the white gaze that surveils her experience, on the collective survival of white supremacy and racism that her story represents, and on the ways in which the teaching and tutoring of academic writing "center[s] a white audience." In footnotes that attend Treviño's critical narrative, Ozias narrates the story of her "listening" to Treviño and models for readers how to "listen." Ozias leads readers by example into the processes of deep reflection, thinking about our own as well as other white women's involvement in racism and white supremacy.

Section Two of *CounterStories* even more closely focuses on stories represented as illegible or made unintelligible in predominantly white writing centres, in which racism and white supremacy are denied or ignored. Each chapter in this section offers a differently nuanced account of the frames and styles of race talk in writing centres that silences, suppresses, that actively harms tutors and administrators of colour.

In chapter 5, "The Stories We Tell and Don't Tell in the Writing Center," Garcia and Kern argue that while the turn to social justice and anti-racism work in the writing center should be celebrated, this celebration should be modulated by a collective recognition of the insufficiency of what we have accomplished. Garcia and Kern assert that with regard to social justice and anti-racism, the writing center does not possess what it professes and does not accomplish what it purports to do. This chapter explores the writing center's overdetermined colonial, ideological, and hierarchical histories and present tenses. Garcia and Kern narrate enactments of white benevolence in the writing centre, its negative effects, and the emotional labor required from People of Color as we/they resist tokenization and, instead, speak out against racial injustice.

The co-authors of chapter 6, "White Benevolence: Why Supa-save-a-Savage Rhetoric Ain't Getting It," Garcia, Faison, and Treviño, explore multiple impacts of whitely epistemologies in the writing center on the Black and Brown tutors and writers. Through the use of autoethnography, Treviño nuances how epistemologies are raced, gendered, and classed. Faison articulates the emotional and intellectual labor required of writing center scholars of colour who embark on anti-racist research and pedagogy in predominantly white writing centers. She discusses her experiences with faulty performances of white alliance as well as the frequent absence of white allies when the attention of scholars of colour turns to racism, white supremacy, and their manifestations in writing centre theory, pedagogy, and tutor education. Finally,

Garcia critiques the ways in which the writing centre is rewritten as colonial and explores how we might begin the process of decolonizing the centre by dis-inventing our pedagogical investments in western epistemologies.

In chapter 7, co-authors Ceballos, Faison, and Olivas testify, each telling one of her own stories about encounters with both primary and secondary racism. That is, each writer narrates not only a direct or explicit experience of racism but also and relatedly an attending experience of denial and silencing performed by white tutors and directors. Ceballos, Faison, and Olivas describe that denial and silencing as "spiritual bypassing," which they define as the practice of "ignoring the racial harm and trauma" of racism on Peoples of Colour.

Section Three features the work of white writing centre scholars and directors who are trying to come to terms with the ways and degrees to which racism and white supremacy manifest and are operative in and through their writing centres, as well as to understand how their lives, their identifications, and performances of self have also been shaped by them.

In chapter 8, "Resisting White, Patriarchal Emotional Labor in the Writing Center," Caswell explores power, privilege, and white heteronormativity in the writing centre. Caswell argues that the nexus of these forces produces affective economies within writing centres that are both normalized and exploitative. The affective economies of writing centres, Caswell suggests, invite, reject, celebrate, and harm tutors and student writers. While prior writing centre scholarship acknowledges emotional labor, Caswell notes, the way in which emotional labour in the writing centre perpetuates affective economies is driven by white, middle class, patriarchal hegemony. As a countermeasure, Caswell considers how writing center directors might redirect and reframe their own emotional labor to shift the grounds of affective economies in service of more racially just writing centers.

Chapter 9, "A Long Path to *Semi*-Woke," features Reglin's narrative and interrogation of her own performance of white benevolence in working with a struggling student of color. As Reglin's story unfolds, she relates her struggle to unlearn the implicit racism that shaped both her white middle-class subject position and her convictions about the fundamental goodness of her work. Once committed to what she now recognizes as colourblind racism, Reglin describes coming to terms with the concomitance of not knowing and claiming to know that attends colourblind ideology as well as with the impacts of not knowing on the tutors and students with whom she worked.

In chapter 10, "Stories of Activist Allies in the Writing Center," co-authors Smith and Baldwin explore their evolving roles as allies conducting activist work by situating themselves in their own histories and stories. Together they explore the question of whether or not or how they can be allies if they do not share the same positionalities and marginalities of other oppressed peoples. Finally, they argue that allyship is an identity position that must be continuously made and remade, visibly and meaningfully. Smith and Baldwin argue that writing centre directors and tutors must be be brave enough, courageous enough that the risks of allyship seem feasible.

A FINAL NOTE

Anti-racism requires of all of us, but particularly those of us who occupy privileged subject positions, including whiteness, that we/they stay even as the going gets hard—especially as the going gets hard—even as we are called to recognize, acknowledge, and address our/their implicatedness in systems and structures of oppression. We hope that you will stay, that you will sit with being called out, that you will hear the ways in which we are all calling you in, and that you will recognize yourselves in the critical self-reflection the writers in this volume model for you.

~WONDERFUL AND FRANKIE

REFERENCES

Corder, J. W. (1985). Argument as emergence, rhetoric as love. *Rhetoric Review, 4*(1), 16–32.

Bell, D. (1992). *Faces at the Bottom of the Well: The Permanence of Racism.* Basic Books.

Bonilla-Silva, E. (2009). *Racism without Racists: Color-Blind Racism and the Persistence of Racial Inequality in America* (3rd ed.). Rowman & Littlefield.

Condon, F. (2012). *I Hope I Join the Band: Narrative, Affiliation, and Antiracist Rhetoric.* Utah State University Press.

Condon, F. & Green, N.A. (2018). *Letters on Moving from Ally to Accomplice: Anti-Racism and the Teaching of Writing* (L.E. Bartlett, S.L. Tarabochia, A.R. Olinger, & M. Marshall, Eds.). WAC Clearinghouse.

Condon, F., Green, N. A., & Faison, W. (2019). *Critical Race Theory and the Work of Writing Centers.* (J. Mackiewicz, R. Babcock, Eds). Routledge.

Delgado, R. (1989). Storytelling for oppositionists and others: A plea for narrative. *Michigan Law Review, 87* (8), 2411–2441.

Delgado Bernal, Delores, Rebecca Burciaga, ad Juditgh Flores Carmona (2002). "Chicana/Latina Testimonios: Mapping the Methodological, Pedagogical, and Political." *Equity and Excellence in Education,* col. 45, no. 3, 2012, pp 363–72.

Denny, H., Mundy, R., Naydan, L.M., Severe, R., & Sicari, A. (Eds). (2018). *Out in the Center: Public Controversies and Private Struggles.* Utah State University Press.

Frye, M. (2001). *White Woman Feminist, 1983–1992.* (B. Boxill, Ed.). Oxford University Press.

Greenfield, L. (2019). *Radical Writing Center Praxis: A Paradigm for Ethical Political Engagement.* Utah State University Press.

Kendi, I. (2017). *Stamped from the Beginning: The Definitive History of Racist Ideas in America.* Bold Print Books. (Original work published 2016.)

Martinez, A. (2020). *Counterstory: The Rhetoric and Writing of Critical Race Theory.* National Council of Teachers of English.

Williams, P. (1992). *The Alchemy of Race and Rights: Diary of a Law Professor.* Harvard University Press.

SECTION ONE

Calling Out/Calling In

1

PROPHETIC ANTI-RACIST ACTIVISM
"Black Prophetic Fire" REIGNITED

Neisha-Anne S. Green

I'M ALIVE!

2017 at the Los Angeles Hope Festival, Rev. Dr. Cornel West is giving a word entitled "Hope is Spiritual Armor for Fighting Righteous Battles." This word remains readily available on bigthink.com for all to grapple with. The video starts. West is bent over leaning in towards his audience, reducing himself to half his size, when he asks "What does it mean to die in order to learn how to live?" There is no instant response from the audience—I started to respond to his question when I realized that in order to be honest with myself, I had to answer something else first. To answer that question I had to first learn "what does it mean to be alive?"

I arrived at the IWCA 2017 conference barely alive and I wasn't fully aware of it. I was truly walking dead, and I don't even watch that show. The ways and weight of the world had reduced me to a decayed form of who I was designed and meant to be. The effects of racism had begun to mummify parts of me, slowly sucking out the parts I loved most about myself while trying to replace and preserve those holy spaces with fear, depression, anxiety, and resentment. With what little I had left, I told the story of Jedidiah Brown, the activist and pastor from Chicago who had attempted suicide under the weight of the world and the work. I confessed that I often wondered about my own mental health and well-being, but I kept the answer and truth to myself. I professed with all the strength I had that Black lives matter. "In Chicago the need to push through my tears kept my dark body from being torn asunder" (2018). On that stage the pieces of my physical body remained somewhat intact, but my emotional and mental form went into arrest and each met their own deaths.

https://doi.org/10.7330/9781646421534.c001

Our trusted Google defines life as

1. The condition that distinguishes animals and plants from inorganic matter, including the capacity for growth, reproduction, functional activity, and continual change preceding death.
2. The existence of an individual human being or animal.

What struck me most were not the definitions on their own, but the synonyms associated with each one. Those synonyms are Existence. Being. Living. Person. Human Being. Individual. Mortal. Soul. Creature.

These words, which were meant to give additional meaning and reference to having life, are missing from our approach to anti-racist work.

This is not a trick question. When you look at me, what do you see? What does my life represent to you? My experiences as I maneuver through the world give me an impression, but I really do wish you could answer this question for me, right now.

I know that these words are missing because I experience it all too often in my everyday life. I've been at American University since the summer of 2016. Keep that in mind when I tell you this story. Back in February of 2019 we invited Asao Inoue come to campus for a full day of workshops for faculty. Before Asao's visit I took part in our campus's annual conference and gave a presentation with the goal of prepping faculty to receive cognitive overload and to be uncomfortable. At the plenary on the day of his visit, I introduced him to the audience and then ran around like a true tech professional handing people the mic so they could ask their questions and tell him how racist they think he is—but that is another story. Despite a few snags I was pleased with the results of the day and most of what I continued to hear throughout the spring semester as folks continued to digest these new ideas. Now, I'm not a one-and-done kind of educator. I prefer to scaffold and keep revisiting and building on ideas so when I was given the opportunity to follow up Asao's visit, I said yes. I decided to co-host a workshop where faculty would be invited to come with their syllabi and rubrics to purposefully work at decolonizing their materials. The goal for the day was to commit to doing any one thing better for all students.

At the end of the workshop I shared that I would be happy to keep thinking on these ideas individually and for those who were interested, I shared a growing reading list Frankie Condon and I had started the summer before to complement our keynote at the International Writing Across the Curriculum conference. We end and a white lady professor walks up to me and says thank you and starts to tell me how much she trusts the writing center because it has been very useful for her students. At this point, I was beaming cause sometimes I am unsure whether I am giving the tutors enough of what they need. I get ready to check this off as a win when she says, "And I'm really glad I came today because I finally get to meet you. I had no idea that the writing center director was Black. All the writing center directors I know are white."

Again, these words are missing from our commitment to this work.

Existence.
Being.
Living.
Person.
Human Being.
Individual.
Mortal.
Soul.

Creature.
We all deserve to EXIST.
We all deserve to BE.
We all deserve to LIVE.
We are all PEOPLE.
We are all HUMAN BEINGS.
We are all INDIVIDUALS.
We all have a SOUL.
We are all MORTAL—which means that we only have but so much time to
    get this right. We only have so much time to exist, to be, to live, to be
    good people, to be better human beings, to be our best selves. To have a
    soul worth remembering.

Cornel West once said, I am who I am cause somebody loved me. I am Neisha-Anne Shanese Green. Daughter of Neville Green and the late Anne Green. I am sister to Neville Andre Green. I am cousin to too many who sometimes call me NeNe. I am niece to Sandra, Joan, Sonia, Charles, Edwin, John, Andy, Jackie and a lot more. I am a friend and an accomplice.

I know who I am so I can call myself Black. But when you point out to me that I am Black, I'm not sure what to do with you or your comment because I gather that you imagine that the color of my skin is a disqualification. I gather that you think that the only qualified tutors, assistant directors, graduate assistants, and directors are white.

In moving with West, when I say I am Black I am keeping track of the historical specificity of a priceless and precious people who had been terrorized, traumatized, and stigmatized by the American nation's state, the economy and large numbers of American citizens. And in reflecting on who they are and on their humanity they were still able in the face of terrorism not to generate counterterrorism, but to call for the freedom of everybody.

Insert, the freedom for a young Black woman like me to be a writing center director because she wanted to be, even though she never saw one who looked liked her. Insert again, the freedom of a person of color to be a writing center director, a writing center tutor, a graduate assistant and whatever the hell they want to be, even if they have never seen anyone who looks like them do the work and better still, even if you have never seen one who looks like them.

I know you're not thinking of me that deeply but because I am who I am, because I know that somebody other than you loves me, and because I was reminded of these things, I choose hope, which is to choose life.

So West asks, "What does it mean to learn to die in order to learn how to live?" West quotes Seneca and then I start to begin to understand where he is going. "Seneca says he or she who learns to die unlearns slavery because . . . deep education, not cheap school—deep education is about critical self-examination of that which is inside of us that needs to die" (2017). You tried to kill me time and time again. Death and I got real close every time you . . . But what you underestimated was the fire shut up in my bones and its redeeming powers.

I restate West's question with you in mind and ask "What is it inside of you that needs to die in order for you to unlearn slavery and racism so that we may get on with the actions of fixing this problem?" I propose a few answers. The hate in you needs to die. The egoism in you needs to die. The fear of yourself needs to die. These things and more need to die so that hope may live. You can more accurately give answer to this question by critically examining yourself and asking am I aware? What am I aware of? What are my biases, both conscious and unconscious? When you have done that, then you are ready for the step after accomplice. You are ready for prophetic anti-racist activism.

To understand prophetic anti-racist activism, one must understand the difference between being a leader and a prophet. West says that, "A leader is somebody who has to jump in the middle of the fray and be prudential, we hope, rather than opportunistic, but a prophetic person tells the truth, exposes lies, [and] bears witness . . ." I see prophetic anti-racist activism as being drastically different from what we have come to know as anti-racist work. Dr. King, Malcolm X, Fannie Lou Hamer, Medgar Evers and Ida B. Wells, just to name a few, were all prophetic anti-racists in my opinion. What elevated them to this point were their levels of awareness, sense of morality and responsibility, uncommon courage, and precise radical candor in the constant face of danger.

Now what I have to say next is specifically for my POC. I asked you to get into this work and stay in it. So, I am doing the same, even though they be trying me. I asked you to challenge Du Bois and revisit our traditional views of double-consciousness and find a way to see and trust your own true consciousness, your own vision of yourself through the haze. With your new true consciousness about you and with the old double-consciousness behind you, I ask you to think carefully on Cornel West. That man is for us, but Lord he be hard on us. His ideas are never popular cause they are like salt in our ancient wounds. But as I digested his words I reminded myself that salt has healing properties. Can we endure a little salt together?

West (2014) salted us real good when he critiqued Black culture and observed what he called a "fundamental shift from a we-consciousness to an I-consciousness [that] reflected not only a growing sense of Black collective defeat but also a Black embrace of the seductive myth of individualism in American culture" (p. 1). Let me repeat that and take this slow cause we need this healing. He said that he has seen a shift in how we exist, in how we navigate life in these troubling United States and we have sacrificed our values. He said that we have moved away from our fundamental values, which are usually grounded in knowing that when we fight we are not fighting for ourselves alone. We are fighting for everybody and all, and we have instead started to embrace the myth that to get ahead in this world, to be accepted in this world, that we have be more I-conscious. We basically went from 1 for all or all for all to 1 for 1. And you know what? He is right. When I think on pillars like Dr. King, Malcolm X, Medgar Evers, and Fannie Lou Hamer I see quite clearly what he means. Our ancestors fought and kept fighting together even when they were tired and scared. They did not compromise. West is warning us that to accept the myth is really to accept the problem of racism, which isn't even ours to accept. James Baldwin, in "Letter from A Region in My Mind" said it differently, but the same nonetheless. He said, "there appears to be a vast amount of confusion . . . , but I do not know many Negroes who are eager to be 'accepted' by white people, still less to be loved by them; they, the blacks, simply don't wish to be beaten over the head by the whites every instant of our brief passage on this planet." We just want to live. The struggle is real and it is hard, but we cannot lose sight of our goals. We cannot compromise. I asked you to get into this work and stay in this work and I am here reminding you to do this work as your true authentic self. Remember that while this world, and specifically this writing center space, wasn't built for us and is still trying to figure out how to evolve to include us,

We exist in it,
We fight in it,
We get hurt in it,
We belong in it,
We matter in it,
We excel in it,
Shit, we can give keynotes in it (2018).

REFERENCES

Baldwin, J. (2019, July). James Baldwin: Letter from a region in my mind. *The New Yorker*. https://www.newyorker.com/magazine/1962/11/17/letter-from-a-region-in-my-mind.

Green, N.A. (2018). Moving beyond alright: And the emotional toll of this, my life matters too in the writing center work. *The Writing Center Journal*, *37*(1), 15–34.

Leigh, C. (2014). *Dr. Cornell West and James H. Cone in conversation: Black prophetic fire* [Video]. YouTube. https://www.youtube.com/watch?v=tLDGVuYmedk.

West, C. (2017). *Big think*, big think. [Video]. Big Think. https://bigthink.com/videos/cornel-west-how-hope-fights-the-banality-of-evil.

West, C. & Buschendorf, C. (2014). *Cornel West on Black prophetic fire*. Beacon Press.

2

DEAR SISTER WHITE WOMAN

Frankie Condon

In the fall of 1993 I swaggered into the SUNY Albany writing center with my imposter syndrome tucked as deeply into the chip on my shoulder as I could get it. The first person I met there was Lil Brannon, a white woman who, with her sweet southern drawl, her subtle wit, and her penetrating intellect, would become my mentor, my supervisor, and the model of who and what I aspired to be as an academic. It was Lil who, on that first day, listened carefully to what I am sure was a long and very self-righteous diatribe and responded only, "You really need to read Elspeth Stuckey's *The Violence of Literacy*." I did, and, unsurprisingly, that book (written by another white woman) became a touchstone for me throughout my doctoral education.

In their 2001 edited collection *The Politics of Writing Centers*, co-editors Jane Nelson and Kathy Evertz (2001) note that "writing center work is heavily gendered" (p. xiii). Continuing, they write that "because more women than men work in writing centers, the writing center is conceptualized in traditional feminine terms" (p. xiii). In 2010, Denny makes the same point, writing "Around the country, many more women serve as directors and professional staffers than men" (Denny, 2010, p.90). As I write this chapter in 2019, women continue to outnumber men in writing centre studies. Collectively, over many years, women have laboured within their home institutions to build and sustain writing centres, in our professional organizations to build and sustain community in the field, and in research and scholarship—to move the field from one dominated largely by lore to a research-driven locus for meaningful and productive one-with-one pedagogy. However, the truth is that it is not merely women whose voices have both shaped and dominated our field, but *white* women. And it is not some generalized or universalized conceptualization "in feminine terms" that has shaped the field, but white femininity.

No credible person, I think, can dispute the extraordinary contributions to the growth and development of writing centre studies by such

https://doi.org/10.7330/9781646421534.c002

luminaries as Tilly Warnock, Lil Brannon, Jeanne Simpson, Muriel Harris, Joan Mullins, and Pam Childers, for example. And no credible person would dispute the significance of both the scholarly and organizational work of Andrea Lunsford, Christina Murphy, Anne DiPardo, Carol Havilland, Meg Carroll, Anne Ellen Geller, Michele Eodice, Shareen Grogan, Jackie Grutsch McKinney, Nancy Welsh, Elizabeth Boquet, Melissa Ianetta, Lauren Fitzgerald, Laura Greenfield, Karen Rowan, Nancy Grimm, Kirsten Jamsen, Katie Levin, Moira Ozias, Beth Godbee . . . I could go on and on and on. No credible person should, I think, doubt the commitment, the hard work, the good intentions of many more white women who attend the field's conferences—moving from session to session, studiously taking notes, and at the end of the day gathering in small enclaves to talk together about the challenges their writing centres face and how to overcome them.

Despite all of our good, hard, well intentioned work, however, we, white women, have not yet offered a full and fair accounting of the field's failure to attract, support, recognize, acknowledge, listen, and, finally, yield—as accomplices or even allies, if that's all we can manage—to women, men, and trans peoples of colour. In her book, *Noise from the Writing Center*, Boquet uses the phrase "high risk/high yield" tutor education. Beth argues against a content-driven approach to the preparation of tutors for one-with-one work with student writers. Such an approach, Boquet suggests, aims to lower the risks associated with not knowing exactly what to say or do, or, as my co-authors and I suggested in *The Everyday Writing Center*, prevent the possibility of being surprised. However inadvertently, risk averse approaches to tutoring in writing also lead to the reaping of fewer rewards—of lowered yield. But we have been risk-averse not only in how we teach tutors to work one-with-one with student writers but also in our stewardship of the field of writing centre studies. In particular, I believe, consciously or unconsciously, we have treated as *risky* the opening of the field and its leadership to women of colour (Queer, and Trans, as well as cis-gendered). I have to admit that I have been kind of obsessed with Beth's use of the term yield for a long time now. I'm intrigued by the manifold meanings of the term:

Yield: produce or provide (this meaning has farming or gardening resonances for me)

Yield: to give way to arguments or pressure, to give up the struggle and surrender

Yield: recognize the right of way of others and get the hell out of the way

Yield: to yield the floor—to give over space, time, and an audience to another

Yes, in 2005 we invited Victor Villanueva to keynote the Minneapolis IWCA conference, where he spoke compellingly of colourblindness as the new racism. And yes, at our Chicago gathering in 2017, Neisha-Anne Green became the first woman of colour to ever keynote an IWCA conference. But attendees at the conference and scholars publishing in the field are still overwhelmingly white. We have not yet yielded in any sense of the term.

The first anti-racism special interest group was organized for the 2007 IWCA conference in Houston by Moira Ozias, Beth Godbee, and me. Although our gathering there was small, the meeting of that first SIG caused some consternation among established writing centre scholars. In 2008, the IWCA conference convened in Las Vegas, Nevada. Fifty people attended the anti-racism SIG at that conference. We gathered in a room designed for, probably, thirty. And we worked! We talked and processed and planned. Folks testified. But outside of that room, the questions came up—again and again and again. Is this really our job? Isn't it really all too much for our tutors? What about teaching "good writing"? Isn't that enough? But student-writers will fail all the things if we don't do what we do the way we know how to do! Isn't it really all too much for us? The SIG has continued to meet at each IWCA conference since 2007, its numbers growing a little, shrinking a little, and then growing again. But the field has not yet yielded.

In 2012, the IWCA recognized Laura Greenfield and Karen Rowan's edited collection, *Writing Centers and the New Racism: A Call for Sustainable Dialogue and Change*, with its best book award. However, as Haltiwanger-Morrison points out in this volume, that book was edited by white women and "features overwhelmingly the voices of White women scholars" (35). In 2019, *Out in the Center: Public Controversies and Private Struggles*, edited by Harry Denny, Robert Mundy, Liliana Haydan, Richard Sévère, and Anna Sicari, was published by Utah State University Press. And, at the 2019 IWCA conference, this book—which does take an intersectional approach to identity matters in the writing center and foregrounds the scholarly work and voices of peoples of colour—was recognized with the best book award by the IWCA. Perhaps, we are moving, however slowly and tentatively, toward yielding. Finally, in 2019, Laura Greenfield's book, *Radical Writing Center Praxis: A Paradigm for Ethical Political Engagement*, was published. In it, Greenfield (2019) encourages, teaches, and cajoles readers to story our writing centre lives as "an immediate, love-inspired, reflective action we commit to again and again and again" (p. 172). More movement.

Recently, I was asked by a young and dedicated writing centre director to help him articulate why anti-racism is significant or necessary to the work of writing centres. I was surprised by the question and then delighted. For this, I think, is exactly the sort of question we want white writing centre folks to ask when they don't know. And so, we talked. Historically, we agreed, the development of writing centres has been associated with the democratization of higher education. Peer tutoring and its locus—the writing centre—were, as Bruffee (1984) pointed out in his pivotal essay "Peer Tutoring and the Conversation of Mankind" [*sic*], cultivated as a way to provide meaningful and productive support to an increasingly diverse student body in North American colleges and universities (p. 207). Further, my new friend and I noted, given the preponderance of scholarship linking language as well as rhetoric to identity (Smitherman 1977; Anzuldua 2012; Villanueva 1993; Young 2007; Richardson 2003; Kynard 2013; Green 2018; Garcia 2017; for example) and English to linguistic supremacy (Phillipson 2015; Sledd 1969; Lu 2013; Horner 2013; Barrett 2008; Smitherman 1973; etc.), it seems absurd to suggest that the work of writing centres is *not* implicated and therefore that writing centre directors, tutors, and scholars are *not* responsible for embedding and enacting anti-racism as a commitment central to our theory and practice. And yet, we are required—those of us who have been doing the work for a long time as well as those of us who are beginning to do the work—to reiterate over and over again why we do what we do, and why we want others to join us. Backsliding.

Wonderful Faison and I, alongside the authors whose work is collected in this volume, have sought, I believe, to sustain what momentum we perceive in the field and to strengthen it. Here, we have sought to put the voices of emerging scholars in writing centre studies who are intersectional feminist women (and men) of colour storying their lived experiences with racism in the writing centre in conversation with those of white women who are contending with what whiteness means and has meant in our lives, for our lives as writing centre directors and scholars. We have attempted to call out and to call in our readers as we call ourselves out and in: to speak out honestly and openly even and especially when rage (eloquent rage, as Brittney Cooper terms it) burns our tongues; to listen well and deeply even and especially when the stories we hear challenge core beliefs about who we are and have been in the world. And we have done this work with the recognition that the expression of rage, frustration, and anguish is not the saboteur of radical love but—when racism and white supremacy are at the table—its enabling conditions.

We have tried—I am trying—to be courageous in articulating my frustration with myself and with other white women in writing centre studies, recognizing, as Deming (2018) has written, that "there is clearly a kind of anger that is healthy. It is the concentration of one's whole being in the determination: this must change." "This kind of anger," she continues,

> is not in itself violent—even when it raises its voice (which it sometimes does); and brings about agitation, confrontation (which it always does). It contains both respect for oneself and respect for the other. To oneself it says: 'I must change—for I have been playing the part of the slave.' To the other it says: 'You must change—for you have been playing the part of the tyrant.' It contains the conviction that change is possible—for both sides; and it is capable of transmitting this conviction to others, touching them with the energy of it—even one's antagonist. (para. 38)

It will come as no surprise to those in the field who have known me and my work that my anger is not a new affect but one that has long simmered. In my relations with student-writers, tutors, with graduate students and emerging scholars, and with my colleagues—who, in this field, have tended to be white women—I have tried to be kind. I have tried to give the best of what and how I think. I have tried to listen well and deeply, to build and sustain affiliations, to recognize and acknowledge the reciprocity of our relations. I have tried to learn from those around me and, actually, I think this is the one attempt at which I have been successful. I have learned so much from so many people who work in and around writing centres. But I have also tried to speak plainly and so I have not kept secret my frustration at the field's general implacability, its insouciance, its molasses-like response to calls from young scholars of colour and their accomplices, like those whose work is collected here, to acknowledge and to act with regard to race matters in our field.

Years ago, I ran for president of IWCA. I ran because I believe in democracy and I didn't think an uncontested election was good for any organization. When the election was over and I had lost, rumours circulated that voting members had been contacted by powerful (white) women in the field and urged not to vote for me because I was "not gracious enough" to fulfill the role for which I was running. I didn't mind losing, but for a long time I struggled with how wounded I felt by that representation of my character. It took months for me to realize that what I should feel wounded about was the suggestion that "graciousness" should be the credentialing criterion for a woman who would be president of the IWCA. And it took years for me to realize that the actual imperative animating a campaign against my candidacy was not merely my lack of graciousness, not only the misogynist notion that women must be "gracious" if they would lead, but an active refusal to consider, let alone do anti-oppression work within the organization and in the field writ large.

In their essay, "Civility and White Institutional Presence: An Exploration of White Students Understanding of Race-Talk at a Traditionally White Institution," C. Kyle Rudick and Kathryn Golsan (2017) write that "hegemonic civility constitutes behaviors that appear appropriate while functioning to silence and oppress marginalized people within educational spaces" (p. 2). Continuing, they note that "hegemonic civility functions to (re)produce White racial power by privileging race-evasiveness, avoiding discussions about race, and excluding of people of color from public spaces" and "perpetuates an oppressive culture in higher education" (p. 2). Hegemonic civility works similarly to police white alliances and allegiance to white domination when activated as the threat of exclusion to whites who begin to ally with marginalized peoples. Consent to the rules of racial standing is compulsory for whites within predominantly white institutions and organizations, and one among a number of means by which this consent is made compulsory is the accusation of incivility. This accusation is particularly pernicious in sabotaging white alliance and accomplice-ship when leveled at white women, for it invokes rules of white gender standing under white patriarchy. As Marilyn Frye (2001) writes, "being rational, righteous, and ruly (rule-abiding, and rule enforcing) do for some of us some of the time buy a ticket to a higher level of material well-being than we might otherwise be permitted (though it is not dependable). But the reason, right, and rules are not of our own making" (15/22). Continuing, Frye writes, "but if our whiteliness[1] commands any respect, it is only in the sense that a woman who is chaste and obedient is called (by classic patriarchal reversal) 'respectable'" (15/22). If nothing else, the rules of white gender standing might help us understand why so many white women have either stood in the way or stood by as tutors, directors, scholars of colour and their accomplices have struggled for change in the field as they help us understand how it is that those white women who have spoken up have been quietly and insidiously ignored, sidelined, or acknowledged and rewarded for anything other than their anti-racism work.

---

1. Marilyn Frye defines and explains whiteliness in her essay, "White Woman Feminist." In brief, she writes that "whitely people generally consider themselves to be benevolent and good-willed, fair, honest, and ethical . . . Whitely people have a staggering faith in their own rightness and goodness, and that of other whitely people" (8/22) and further that "change cannot be initiated unless the moves are made in appropriate ways. The rules are often rehearsed" (9/22).

Civility, conceived and practiced as the enforcement of whiteliness, disguises a great number of sins, I've come to believe. For white women, civility has served as an exceptionally effective veil not only for distaste, frustration, and anger, but also for rage. I've come to believe that, generally speaking, the more polite a white woman becomes in conflict situations, the angrier she is. And so, I have come to believe that I am not the only white woman in the field of writing centre studies who is angry. Some of us, however, are angry for different reasons.

In her essay on intersectionality, published in *The Oxford Handbook of Feminist Theory*, Brittney Cooper (2019) writes that "while intersectionality should be credited with 'lifting the veil,' to invoke Du Bois's metaphor of the racial 'color line,' we should remain clear that the goal of intersectionality is not to provide an epistemological mechanism to bring communities from behind the veil into full legibility. It is rather to rend the veil and make sure that no arguments are articulated to support its reconstruction" (9/23). And so, from the white side of the colour line, and in the name of "snatching my people," as Neisha-Anne Green might say, I propose to unveil in the most direct way I can think of my anger not only at myself (for I am perpetually angry at myself for the whiteliness that will creep into my thinking, my speaking, my acting no matter how hard I try to expel it) but at so many white women in writing centre studies who have refused, categorically, to lean in, to listen, and especially to stay—even through the hardness of the conversations it engenders—with anti-racism. Of course, real anger, real rage are most fierce when we are disappointed in those we love. And so, this is the letter—the diatribe, the love letter, the expression of both bitter disappointment and abiding love—that I have written and rewritten, written and rewritten over two decades of writing centre work, but never sent. I send it now.

Dear Sister White Woman,
I hope you aren't offended by me calling you sister—it's just that I feel that I know you almost as well as I know myself.

Dear Sister White Woman, I truly don't mean to offend—I know we grew up, you and me, on the story of our uniqueness and we've invested, well, not just you and me but our mothers and grandmothers, aunties and sisters, for generation after generation we have all invested quite a bit of energy establishing our exceptionalism

such that to call you sister, to tell you, baby, I recognize the quick flush that rises from your neck to your cheeks before you can check it, push it down, call it something—anything—other than what it is

white hot rage

to say I know how to read that sign might suggest to you that we are not so different from one another, might remind you that in our heart of hearts we are not *all* the same but our life is composed of days traversing the same sticky web of lies we've been so well trained to keep on spinning, to believe, to use to catch all the Others and bind them up as well, to enforce and to pass on

to say I know you is to say I have seen us act this way before, I have heard us speak these words before

. . . and I am seeing pattern in the web I just wanna talk about . . . can you just, can you just, can you just stay with me while I tell you I have seen this all before

I get it. You're angry. You're pissed. You're outraged. You're shocked and appalled and angry. You're so fucking mad you can't even.

But sister, please tell me, for whom is your anger a gift?

I ask because what I see, what I see is an act—it's theatre—and like any play the lines we run when we are acting up are designed not so much so we can be what we say, but so we can seem like what we want to be seen as being.

You're confused. You don't know what I mean. Well, it's just this:

Here's an obvious example: Imagine: You're invited to offer some account of white privilege—to acknowledge, to own up, or just to take an itty bitty sideways glance at the possibility that whatever we got, you and me, by walking through the world in this skin we didn't earn

You say, "How dare you?! You have made me . . . uncomfortable . . . I'm taking my shit and going home!" And right there, baby, you just gave a gift to white privilege. In denying it exists and asserting your right to exercise it all at the same time, you made it real. And what keeps it real is the day after day, moment after moment, sister after sister performance of that script.

Here's an ugly one—a particularly pernicious one—your friend gets called out cuz she's said or done a thing that wounds; she's acted unthinkingly, mindlessly maybe, she's spooled out some racism or other. And she stands up. And she says, "you're right. I take responsibility and I commit to you and to myself that I will study, I will learn, I will figure out, by God, how to be right . . . somehow . . ." And any fool can see she needs help to learn because no one can do this work alone. And you say to her, you say "SHH-HHHHHHHHHH." You mob her, then you shun her cuz she broke the code of silence when she said "this is real." But you know, and I know you know her real crime was reminding you of the things you've said and done and gotten a pass on somehow and of the truth that you weren't brave or honest or humble or kind or fucking human enough to own up.

Then there's this one: You sit back in all the places where sister white women can be observed doing all the sister white women things and you say, "Oh yes, those OTHER white women—I *hate* those OTHER white women." And what you mean is, "That's not me cuz I'm a better sort of white woman." And what you've done right there is to absolve yourself of all the wickedness the idea of whiteness does in the world—to say there's a category of whiteness worth preserving and it is me.

No, wait. Don't go yet! You're gonna love this one: Your friend gets called out cuz she's said or done a thing that wounds; she's acted unthinkingly, mindlessly maybe, she's spooled out some racism or other.

And you say, to anyone who will listen, as loud as you can, you trumpet, baby, how down low and bad you think she is. She's so bad! You say it over and over, **but never to her**. You never snatch your people up and school them the way we would do if we understood that that's our job. You just keep saying, SHE'S SO BAD! And underneath all that shouting, what's really under there, is how bad you want the approval of People of Colour, how much you want to be loved or liked or something, you want favoured nation status—so much so that you'd abdicate doing the work of taking your sister aside for tough love in favour of being heard despising her <u>as if you aren't her</u>.

Oh, I could go on. But here's my point: can't we just, you and me ask ourselves, for whom are these performances of anger a gift?

Barbara Deming says there is an anger that is an affliction—an affliction, she says, that "asserts to another not: 'you must change and you can change'—but: 'your very existence is a threat to my very existence.' " This anger, she says, "speaks not hope but fear. The fear is you can't change—and I can't change if you are still here." This anger, Deming says, "asserts not: change! But: drop dead!"

And there's a difference between that anger and the righteous anger that as Barbara Deming says, concentrates "one's whole being in the determination: this must change."

But there's also a difference, my love, my friend, my heart, between righteous anger and the self-righteous anger that says "it is more important for me to appear to be goodness and righteousness personified than to do the work of antiracism."

Our self-righteous anger, my love, enables us to avoid the necessity of confronting our own fragility and confounding it.

Our self-righteous anger is the gift we give ourselves and like every gift this one comes with a demand or a plea or an expectation of reciprocity. You look this gift horse in the mouth and what you got is—you will continue to be a functionary for racism.

Can we just be honest for a minute? Our self-righteous anger is our attempt to resurrect a white woman whose whiteness is worth saving. **But I say to you now that from within the crucible of racism the work is to resurrect a woman whose humanity is worth saving**.

Our self-righteous anger is the exit ramp from doing our own work on our own selves; and from taking responsibility for one another, snatching our people with that quick, hard, and loving snap that says STOP NOW and I will stay with you while we figure out what just happened right there and how to not do that again.

Sister, my love, the real gift in those moments when I hate what I have done, what you have done, what our people have wrought or you hate me would be that rage that is conditioned by love and by commitment: I will not build my status as an antiracist accomplice on your back, but stay in the in-between with you where we can teach each other a thing or two. Will you be that with me?

Love,
frankie

REFERENCES

Anzuldua, G. (2012). *Borderlands/La Frontera: The New Mestiza* (4th ed.). Aunt Lute Books.

Barrett, R., Young, V.A., Young-Rivera, Y., & Lovejoy, K.B. (2018). *Other People's English: Code-Meshing, Code-Switching, and African American Literacy*. Parlour Press. (Original work published 2014)

Bruffee, K. (1984). Peer tutoring and the conversation of mankind (R. Barnett and J.S. Blumner, Eds). *The Longman Guide to Writing Center Theory and Practice* (pp. 206–218). Pearson.

Cooper, B. (2018). *Eloquent rage*. St. Martin's Press.

Cooper, B. (2019). Intersectionality. *The Oxford Handbook of Feminist Theory*. Oxford University Press.

Demming, B. (2018 Jan.). On anger. *Peace News*. https://peacenews.info/node/7610/anger%EF%BB%BF.

Denny, H. (2010). *Facing the Center: Toward an Identity Politics of One-to-One Mentoring*. Utah State University Press.

Denny, H., Mundy, R., Naydan, L.M., Severe, R., & Sicari, A. (2018). *Out in the Center: Public Controversies and Private Struggles*. Utah State University Press.

DiPardo, A. (1992). Whispers of coming and going. *The Writing Center Journal, 12*(2), 125–144.

Frye, M. (1992). *Willful Virgin: Essays in Feminism*. Crossing Press.

Garcia, R. (2017). Unmaking gringo centers. *The Writing Center Journal, 36*(1), 29–60.

Green, N.A. (2018). Moving beyond alright: And the emotional toll of this, my life matters too in the writing center work. *The Writing Center Journal, 37*(1), 15–34.

Greenfield, L. (2019). *Radical Writing Center Praxis: A Paradigm for Ethical Political Engagement*. Utah State University Press.

Greenfield, L., & Rowan, K. (2011). *Writing Centers and the New Racism: A Call for Sustainable Dialogue and Change*. Utah State University Press.

Grimm, N. M. (1999). *Good Intentions: Writing Center Work for Postmodern Times*. Boynton/Cook.

Kynard, C. (2013). *Vernacular Insurrections: Race, Black Protest, and the New Century in Composition-Literacies Studies*. SUNY Press.

Lassner, P. (1994). "The politics of otherness: Negotiating distance and difference" (J. Mullins and R. Wallace, Eds). *Intersections: Theory-practice in the Writing Center* (pp. 148–160). NCTE.

Lu, M.Z., & Horner, B. (2013). Translingual literacy, language difference, and matters of agency. *College English, 75*(6), 582–607.

Mullins, J. and Wallace, R. (1994). *Intersections: Theory-Practice in the Writing Center*. NCTE.

Nelson, J. and Evertz, K. (2001). *The Politics of Writing Centers*. Boynton/Cook.

The Oxford Handbook of Feminist Theory. (2019). Oxford University Press.

Phillipson, R. (2015). *Linguistic Imperialism*. Routledge.

Richardson, E. (2003). *African American Literacies*. Routledge.

Rudick, K.C. & Golsan, K.B. (2017). Civility and white institutional presence: An exploration of white students understanding of race-talk at a traditionally white institution. *Howard Journal of Communications*, 1–18.

Sledd, J. (1969). Bi-dialectalism: the linguistics of white supremacy. *The English Journal 58*(9), 1307–29.

Smitherman, G. (1973). White English in blackface, or who do I be? *The Black Scholar, 4*(8/9), 32–39.

Smitherman, G. (1977). *Talkin and Testifyin: The Language of Black America*. Houghton Mifflin.

Villanueva, V. (1993). *Bootstraps: From an American Academic of Color*. NCTE.

Young, V.A. (2007). *Your Average Nigga: Performing Race, Literacy, and Masculinity*. Wayne State University Press.

3

BEYOND THE BINARY
Revealing a Continuum of Racism in Writing Center Theory and Practice

Talisha Haltiwanger Morrison

The field of writing centers may be experiencing, or perhaps be in need of, an identity crisis. The scholarship on conflict, tension, and disagreement in writing centers is plentiful: Who are we? Where did we come from? What is our purpose? How do we do what we do? (Denny, 2010; Boquet, 1999; McKinney, 2013). While the field is still engaging in these conversations, some within it have decided to go deeper, to talk about the elephant in the center: racism. The field of writing center studies has been experiencing a turn towards anti-racism, taking up critical race theory in its scholarship and engaging in regular conversations among its professionals about how to combat racism in our centers. The conversation, in large part due to the demographics of the field, has been dominated by white people, particularly white women. One place this is made particularly evident is in the 2011 edited collection, *Writing Centers and the New Racism* (Greenfield & Rowan), which features overwhelmingly the voices of white women scholars. The white female voices currently shaping conversations on writing centers and race are well-meaning. As Nancy Grimm (1999) would say, they have "good intentions." But "well-meaning" does not mean "not racist." I contend that well-meaning white women writing center directors enact racism and do so regularly. They do so directly and indirectly, through action and through passivity. I offer examples of a lack of racial awareness among white women, manifested through real life interactions and through the field's scholarship and call for shifting our conception of racism to a continuum and for a commitment to increased racial awareness amongst white writing center professionals.

Barbara Trepagnier (2010) discusses the racism of well-meaning whites, specifically well-meaning white women, in her book, *Silent Racism: How Well-Meaning White People Perpetuate the Racial Divide*. Trepagnier

https://doi.org/10.7330/9781646421534.c003

argues that most white people fundamentally misunderstand modern racism and racists, dividing (white) people into two categories: "racist" and "not racist." These categories "hide subtle acts of racism, especially from the actors performing them." This is because the "'not racist' category implies no harm is done" (p. 5). Trepagnier argues in favor of a continuum of "more racist" to "less racist" in place of the two oppositional categories, which might make silent racism, or "unspoken, negative thoughts, emotions, and assumptions about black Americans that dwell in the minds of white Americans, including well-meaning whites that care about racial equality" (p. 15). I believe Trepagnier's continuum, as well as the concept of silent racism, are useful concepts for writing center practitioners to understand how racism operates in our centers and institutions.

Below I share an illustrative example, originally shared with me during a different project (Haltiwanger Morrison, 2018), experienced by a Black woman tutor named Fatou, who works in a center with two white directors, one male, one female. I provide analysis of this experience as a time when silent racism and spoken racism worked to maintain racist norms of writing centers and institutions generally. I follow this analysis with personal narrative and analysis of responses I received after sharing Fatou's experience at a research conference, an interaction which ironically reflected the racism I had just described and critiqued. Additionally, it is of note that all of the white people in the experiences I recount below would almost certainly place themselves in the "not racist" category of the binary. However, through analysis, it becomes clear why a continuum is more appropriate and useful for understanding racist actions.

Fatou is a writing tutor at a large public research institution PWI (predominantly white institution) in the Northeast. She is a first-generation Guinean-American who identifies as Black and African American. During one of our conversations, Fatou shared the following experience:

> There was this one incident that kind of blew up . . . I think [our directors] asked how can we better—how can we upkeep professionalism in the center, because it's really easy for people to fall into their relaxed positions and not take their jobs really seriously because we are student employees and we don't have a dress code or anything . . . But, umm, she [a white grad student] mentioned everyone wearing their name tags, which we have, and they're really nice, so I was like, yeah, of course, you should wear your name tag. But her reasoning behind it was because "*some* of us have unusual names," and we should wear our name tags so people can see our names. One, just because you see my name tag doesn't mean you can read it, but when she said "unusual names," she shot her eyes over at me, and

the Indian girl beside me, and the Arabian girl beside me, too. So, in that section, she looked at that section and immediately said "unusual names," which one, I'm used to being told because my name isn't from this country, so I know that it's not typical of White Americans, that makes sense to me. But to call it "unusual" is not okay.

Fatou approached the graduate tutor in private a few days after the incident to express her concern over the comment and to explain that she and some of the other tutors of color had been offended. The white tutor became defensive and refused to apologize, insisting that the comment was not about race or culture, that she only meant people should wear their name tags at work. This argument made little sense to Fatou because as she explains,

> but if my name is "unusual," or atypical of this culture, what would wearing my name tag really accomplish? Because if you can't read "Fatou" on paper, you can't read "Fatou" when you're setting up your appointment, what makes you think you can read "Fatou" when it's on my chest, on my name tag? And, she really couldn't answer the question, so I just made it clear that it was offensive to me and to other people, I just would hope that, even if she didn't mean anything offensive by it, [her] word choice is really deliberate, and particularly working in the writing center, you know what words can do and how they can change situations and how the connotation can be. And so, I didn't have time to keep dealing with her defensiveness, particularly with everything that I was expressing to her, coming to her as a person who wasn't necessarily a tutor, but someone who was disrespected because my, for most of my academic life, my name has been considered to be weird, so that was taken into account, and then I went and talked to other undergraduates, because we were the only other ones of color [laughs], and we went to one of the directors at the time, and then we had an emergency meeting.

This incident started out with what might appear to many reading this as a blatantly racist comment by a white woman graduate tutor, a comment about Fatou's name, which is tied to her ethnicity and culture. Wrapped in the guise of "professionalism," this racism is not silent, but what Villanueva (2006) terms the "new racism," a linguistic shift to shield the nature of the conversation. This shift allows the white tutor to deny, or perhaps to genuinely not see the racist nature of her comment. It allows her to place herself in the "not racist" category because she is not talking about "race." I would not identify this comment as a form of "silent racism," as, for one, it is spoken. Rather, I would consider it as what Jane Hill (2009) terms the everyday language of white racism. Hill offers a framework of linguistic ideologies, and explains that "A central function of language ideologies in the reproduction of white racism is that they make some kinds of talk and text visible as racist, and others invisible" (p. 39). Stereotypes, considered to be false, are visible as racist. Comments coded in the ambiguous language of professionalism are less visibly so. But Hill points to another linguistic ideology, a performative ideology, which Fatou addresses in her confrontation with the white tutor. According to Hill, performative ideology is an ideology "shared by most Americans [and that] holds that words have an active force, that they can soothe or wound." Performative ideology is about "how language makes people feel" and makes it possible to understand some words as "assaultive, rather than as true or false" (p. 40). Realizing that the white tutor cannot see the racism embedded in her language, and confronted with the tutor's defensiveness at the suggestion that her words were offensive, Fatou makes a different kind of appeal, through a different type of filter, as a fellow writing tutor and person who is mindful of the power of language to do harm, intended or not.

Those who work in writing centers might be expected to have greater awareness of these linguistic ideologies. Racist language should be visible as such, and some language should be clearly assaultive. But this is often not the case, in large part because writing centers at PWIs are largely staffed by white people. And they are white people in writing centers at institutions that never anticipated a need to examine such language, because there were few or no People of Color around to be offended or even notice it. While diversity remains low at many PWIs such as Fatou's, it is growing, and regardless of numbers, students and tutors of color deserve to be heard and to have their voices validated. Because she seemed to be making no progress with the white tutor herself, Fatou took the issue to one of her directors, someone with more authority whom she assumed would view her feelings as valid. Her director, a white woman, did take Fatou's concerns seriously, and called a staff meeting to discuss the situation.

Fatou explained that, during the meeting, she and the other undergraduate tutors of color "kinda looked more towards the director to handle things, because that's *their job* to do so." However, she felt the meeting was ultimately not as helpful for her because, although the director took the action of calling the meeting, she remained fairly quiet throughout most of it, while the white female graduate tutor continued to defend her position, and became very upset at having to explain the meaning of her words. Fatou described the other tutors as "emotionally distraught" and said she "felt she was being attacked." Mamta Motwani Accapadi (2007) explains this phenomenon in her piece, "When White women cry: How White women's tears silence women of color." Accapadi provides an intersectional analysis, explaining how white women are able to shift between their "one up/one down" identities as white and women, one identity being privileged, the other not. The subject position of white women as pure because of their powerlessness in relation to white men gives them status over women of color, who do not have a privileged racialized identity to rely on. Another tutor from Fatou's center, whom I also interviewed for my project, also stated that the meeting got out of hand, and the director never stepped in or tried to steer the conversation to a more productive space. She remains a passive bystander (Trepagnier, 2010), and the white tutor leaves the meeting feeling that she is the one who has been wronged.

While some whites remain bystanders because they feel the person experiencing injustice deserves that injustice, others do so out of loyalty or fear of embarrassing or upsetting the perpetrator (p. 49). It is possible that the director felt calling the meeting was action enough, that she had validated Fatou's experience and created opportunity for dialogue. I cannot say exactly what her thought process was, but from Fatou's perspective, her concerns were not given equal opportunity to be heard. When bystanders remain silent, when they choose passivity, they align themselves with the aggressor, and also do harm. It is for this reason that we must understand the falseness of the "racist"/ "not racist" binary. It is imperative that well-meaning whites realize that passivity does harm itself. You cannot say "I'm not racist" if you stand idly by while racism happens right before you. Neither of Fatou's directors (the man or woman) took action after the initial comment, which put the onus on Fatou to seek out the white tutor and defend her identity against racialized attacks in the workspace they oversee. When her own efforts were unsuccessful, she sought out the authority of her boss, only to have that boss remain silent during a conversation seemed to be at best useless, and at worst, to leave the white tutor as the victim, while Fatou's concerns remained unaddressed. Fatou's director was unprepared to do meaningful anti-racist work.

I shared Fatou's experience and others during a presentation at the 2017 International Writing Centers Association Conference, which, like its larger organization, is overflowing with well-meaning whites. Upon conclusion of my talk and those of the other session presenters, I received several questions and comments from interested members of the audience. One woman, a white female director, identified herself as a director at an HBCU (historically Black college or university). The woman, who most likely had mostly good intentions, if perhaps mixed with a bit of righteousness, explained how, at her institution, the Black students experienced racism from their Black faculty members. Seeing that the woman had a flawed understanding of racism, I responded that the tensions between students and faculty at the institution were not due to racism, but may be due to generational differences. Unsatisfied with my response, the woman proceeded to explain to me why the students were in fact experiencing racism because of the names the older professors used in reference to them. She insisted that if *she* were to make these comments, they would be considered racist. A fellow audience member (a white man) jumped in, contributing that the identity of the speaker was important and made a difference. Others (particularly, I noticed, Black women) nodded in agreement with this statement. I explained as well that what the woman was witnessing was not racism. Black people could discriminate and hold prejudices, but racism was something different, a system of power only white people had access to. The woman persisted, becoming, from my perspective, a little defensive, and attempting to explain to me racism: what it was, and why certain things were or were not racism. Despite my efforts to explain, based on my lived experience and research, which I had just presented, my reasoning that the Black people at her institution were not being "racist" to one another, this woman believed she was well informed, believed she was in the right to educate me on racism, believed, I think, she was being helpful, at least at the beginning, before it became clear that no one in the room was going to (outwardly) agree with her. The entire conversation provided further evidence that "Liberal and progressive whites, despite their good intentions, are neither well informed about the historical and cultural impact of racism on blacks nor clear about what is racist" (Trepagnier, 2010, p. 44).

Just like the white tutor from Fatou's experience, my audience member was unable, perhaps unwilling, to see her current actions as racist. As someone who worked closely with a predominantly Black student population and who showed interest in issues of racism and anti-racism, she most likely would place herself in the "not racist" category. After all, the conversation began with her attempting to provide a sort of defense of her students from their Black faculty. And yet, here she was, undermining both my research and my lived experience (which are linked), completely unaware that she was doing it. She was so wrapped in her discussion *about* Black people, that she could not pause and consider that she was in a conversation *with* a Black person, and what that might mean.

A similar phenomenon occurs frequently in real life and in our field's scholarship, when white scholars write *about* Black people and other People of Color, but not *with* or even *to*. I mentioned *Writing Centers and the New Racism* as one text that does not meaningfully or substantially engage the voices of women of color only because it is a well-known text. However, there is very little research in our field that does engage these voices. While white scholars are interested in speaking about racism, they have not made significant efforts to draw in the voices of those most affected by it, student, tutor, or administrator. The failure of white scholars to amplify the voices of women or People of Color in the field means that little of the scholarship in writing center studies, even that on racism and anti-racism, speaks to experiences like mine and Fatou's. And yet, when sharing the story of another Black woman in the field, a tutor, I received comments asking me to "engage more writing center scholarship." This feedback was infuriating in its casual whiteness, in how it overlooked that there was (is) no current scholarship in the field that spoke to the particular experience of this Black, female tutor. It is frustrating that so many do not notice such a gap, not in Greenfield and Rowan's (2011) book, but in our scholarship more generally. Greenfield and Rowan's book is not the problem; the problem is those speaking, and those reading, take no notice of who has and has not had opportunity to speak.

I should clarify that I am not claiming that there is no scholarship in the field by women and People of Color. That is not true. However, most of this work is fairly recent, and our representation on both the pages of our journals and at our conferences is limited. Additionally, when women of color do attend and share our perspectives at conferences, we may have experiences like the one I shared, when a white audience member attempted to explain racism to me, or like what happened immediately after, when one of my fellow presenters, also a white woman, interrupted me and ended the question-and-answer segment, claiming that we were out of time (we were the last panel of the day, and although it was late, no one seemed in a hurry to leave. In fact, many people stayed even later to continue talking). At the time, I was so caught off guard by the move that I could not process that I had just been effectively silenced in an effort to protect the white audience member from further engagement with me. I can only assume that my fellow presenter felt I was being hostile or aggressive. Why else would she need to swoop in and intervene? Although the woman in the audience was not crying, the defensive emotional state she presented allowed her to successfully position herself as the victim, and my fellow panelist sensed her distress and came to the rescue.

I did not have opportunity to address the incident with either woman, as I engaged in further conversation with audience members interested in my work, as well as with the third presenter, another woman of color, and both women had left by the time I wrapped up my conversations. But what stands out from this incident is that a woman who almost certainly would place herself in the "not racist" category instinctively reacted with racism. The research and message I had just delivered had not mattered. Her own research about Black people had not mattered. Her actions demonstrate how silent racism is enacted in ways unnoticed by those performing the racist acts. Because silent racism and individual action are linked with institutional racism (Trepagnier, 2010, p. 81) in doing so, in silencing me, her individual act (at an institutional function) during a moment of institutional critique, worked to maintain institutional racism and the status quo.

What can we extrapolate from the experiences shared here, mine and Fatou's? Based on our interactions with four white women, one graduate tutor and three directors, can it be said that white women in writing centers generally fail to see their racism, are unable and often unwilling to see it? I argue yes. I argue that white women in writing centers are not special, they are not an altogether different breed from other white women, and these are only a few of many stories to be told, of even those I could tell. Those who work in writing centers are educated, and may even have relatively high levels of racial awareness. But race awareness is not itself enough to prevent racist actions (Trepagnier, 2010, p. 35). That much is evidenced by the white presenter who silenced me and protected another white woman, moments after giving a talk about racism against Black people, especially women. Knowing *about* racism is not enough. If white women are unable or unwilling to see their own racism, then they are unable to do effective anti-racist work. I do not think many are willing to do this work if it means confronting the uncomfortable truth of their racism.

What I am asking of well-meaning white women and white scholars in the field more generally is, most simply put, to get over it. I do not mean to suggest at all that this is easy. I am asking well-meaning whites who are committed to anti-racism, or even to doing no harm, to embrace the discomfort that occurs when we let go of the "racist"/ "not racist" binary and understand racism as a spectrum. Trepagnier's book is intended for well-meaning whites because she sees them as the group most likely to receive her argument, to accept that they, too, are capable of racism and to make efforts to change (p. 6). Again, I believe that those in writing centers are not unlike well-meaning whites in other areas. I know because I have been mentored by them, because they are involved in this book project, that there are white scholars and practitioners in the field who are currently doing meaningful anti-racist work. Some of them are even contributors to *Writing Centers and the New Racism.* I am asking well-meaning white women to do thoughtful, genuine anti-racist work by first fully acknowledging racism, including their own. I am asking them to listen for racism, and to listen very closely, because it may be very quiet.

REFERENCES

Boquet, E.H. (1999). "Our little secret": A history of writing centers, pre- to post-open admissions. *College Composition and Communication, 50*(3), 463–682.

Denny, H.C. (2010). *Facing the Center: Toward an Identity Politics of One-on-One Tutoring.* Logan, UT: Utah State University Press.

Greenfield, L., & Rowan, K. (2011). *Writing Centers and the New Racism: A Call for Sustainable Dialogue and Change.* Logan, UT: Utah State University Press.

Grimm, N. M. (1999). *Good Intentions: Writing Center Work for Postmodern Times.* Portsmouth, NH: Heinemann.

Haltiwanger Morrison, T. M. (2018). *Nooses and Balancing Acts: Reflections and Advice on Racism and Antiracism from Black Writing Tutors at Predominantly White Institutions.* (Doctoral dissertation). Retrieved from ProQuest Dissertations and Theses.

Hill, J. H. (2008). *The Everyday Language of White Racism.* Chichester, West Sussex, UK: Wiley-Blackwell.

McKinney, J. G. (2013). *Peripheral Visions for Writing Centers.* Boulder, CO: University Press of Colorado.

Trepagnier, B. (2016). *Silent Racism: How Well-Meaning Whites Perpetuate the Racial Divide* (2nd ed.). New York, NY: Routledge.

Villanueva, V. (2006). Blind: Talking about the new racism. *Writing Center Journal, 26*(1), 3–19.

4

A NEED FOR WRITING COALITIONS
A (Ch)Xicana's Fotos y Recuerdos—Anticipating (Dis)Identification

Anna K. Treviño and Moira Ozias

C. A. Elenes (2000) argues that "Chicana feminist narratives do not portray the self in isolation from the community or from the social structures that reproduce unequal relations of power. Rather, Chicana feminist narratives are manifestations of and struggles against multiple forms of oppression" (p. 105). I agree and therefore consider the words that follow a (Ch)Xicana feminist narrative of mine. In part it is also a testimonio, a counterstory, a part of my ongoing healing process, and an attempt to build academic kinship with the reader. In addition, as I wrote in a Twitter thread of mine, one of my goals is to "de-center the idea of the default audience being white and middle class . . ." because People of Color (PoC) "aren't just not considered a valid audience. The act of denying them as valid audiences actively reproduces the dynamics of power that label them powerless and denies their agency—implying that [PoC] can't be agents for change" (Treviño, 2018b). Thus, because of my goals and the work I have undertaken in this piece, I expect that at times readers will move in and out of identifying or disidentifying with me. This is also intentional. Critically reflect on those moments. Particularly for white readers, but open to all, is Moira's guidance on how to do so in the footnotes. The seventh footnote is one I've written for all readers.

———

"Anna," I remember my mother sharing with mi familia a few weeks before my high school graduation, "was the only one of my kids that actually wanted to go to school, que quería aprender." At some point, while in high school, I remember my mother telling me that my dad's family said they "were surprised we (my two older Treviño brothers and I) did so well at school," especially since we weren't in the RGV (Rio Grande Valley).

https://doi.org/10.7330/9781646421534.c004

Before that, while growing up, I frequently heard my mom tell others that we "must have got it from our dad," because she was never good at school.

From what little my mother has told me, she grew up extremely poor en el rancho. If they (she and her sisters) wanted to play with dolls, I remember her telling me, they would shape a towel to have body-like features (arms, legs, a head), and if they went to the store and needed new shoes for school, they'd buy what they could, even if the shoes were too small. Ultimately, my mother's educational journey (or lack thereof?) as a Mexican-American girl born in 1961 in a small Texas border town, as one of the oldest in a poor family, ended with her eighth grade graduation. "Eighth grade," she says first in this memory I hold, briefly followed by "I was in special ed." I don't remember how old I was when she told me this, but I do know I was at least in high school, past the eighth grade. It was an unexpected thing to hear, but not exactly surprising considering the times my brothers and I had been asked how to spell words in our house, the times I saw the mistakes in the notes she would write to the school when I missed class, the fact that she didn't sound like my teachers when she spoke, the way she pushed the importance of education on to me, and the many I times I heard her tell others that "we got it from our dad." It was painful to hear because I knew even as a teen that the system was not built to help those in poverty succeed.

My father did not grow up poor. Locally, within the population and culture of our U.S.-Mexico border towns, today I would say his family's socio-economic status was solidly middle-class, but nationally, it was upper working-class. That is, the cultural aspects of what is considered middle-class across the U.S. are not the same in the Borderlands. My father, with his associate's degree in construction from Texas State Technical College (TSTC) Edinburg, was on the cusp of middle-classness. But it never happened. He held blue-collar jobs most of his life—rough hands, sweaty caps, tanned skin, muddy steel-toed boots. However, I do remember him saying he worked as a substitute science teacher for a little bit, once. I don't think anyone could say for certain why he "didn't make it," but my guess is that it had something to do with the fact that he, unlike his parents and siblings, was the only one to move away from home, to live in predominantly white small towns.

I wrote pieces of this narrative sitting in a R1 university's writing center, writing between the time I spent working with writers, wondering whether I could actually pass my PhD comprehensive exams in the fall. Remembering the days in the cotton fields. My family of migrant

workers. Wondering how I even got here. How as a kid I grew up playing in the dirt or waiting in the cars during hot ass summers while my
family chopped the weeds in cotton rows that were miles long. I'd take
them water when they needed. There were no bathrooms out there, and
we were out there before the sun was even up. I remember the smell of
the dirt, the morning dew, the sound of crickets and grasshoppers, the
sound of the azadones, grubbing hoes, scraping along the ground, and
the sound of the weeds being torn out. I remember waking up to the
smell of tortillas with my family dressed in long sleeved shirts and caps,
the handkerchiefs, and the sound of ice being poured into ice chests
and filled with water. I remember how everyone huddled to eat and talk
during the quick lunch break, the music, and how some people would
honk as they drove by. I remember the sound of the azadones being
loaded into the trucks, the dirt and sweat.[1] Believe it or not, I wanted to
be chopping weeds instead of waiting for our family to call the day done.
It wasn't work that I ever considered embarrassing.

As a child of migrant workers, I attended many schools, more than a
handful before I reached the sixth grade. After the fourth grade, when
we never returned to South Texas, I overwhelmingly had white women
as teachers, with a few white men. The three times I had teachers of
color in high school, we didn't call them Ms. or Mr. They went by
"coach" outside and inside of the classroom. But in moving from the
domains of a Mexican (American?) home and white school as a child, I

---

1. I'm remembering here my own family's relation to the land, to colonization, and
to race. My mom's family were Swedish immigrants in the late 1800s. They settled
Cheyenne and Arapaho lands right after the U.S. Army massacred hundreds of
women and children across the plains, and specifically at the Sand Creek Massacre,
just south of where my family occupies land. But my family doesn't tell the story start-
ing then. We tell stories about our family's hard-working, "pioneering" history. All
Indigenous histories and connections to the land and place are erased and silenced
completely. No mention of the blood money that came to us via the bits of wealth we
accumulated from colonizing the land. My family made money by owning land, living on that land, working it with increasingly elaborate and expensive technologies.
(Have you seen a modern combine or harvester? There's nothing azadone-like about
these $400,000 moving computers.)

I could make connections between Anna's memories of coolers and sounds of ice,
long days in the fields, the smell of dirt and sounds of crickets and grasshoppers, but
while we both have these connections to land, our relations to it are in every way different. I have a grief about that, and a guilt that I try to turn to anger. Being angry at
my ancestors is complicated, but feels necessary if I'm to become what Marie Battiste
calls "response-able" to Indigenous communities, and to the folks of color I live with,
work with, and love.

learned other things: English was for school and Spanish was for home, what happened at school was education and the key to success, who I was outside of school, with my family, my culture didn't matter *as much.*

"Every time you speak, it makes me want to cry," I told a Latina professor. She was a bit taken aback, thinking I meant her words offended or hurt my feelings. "No, it's that I don't realize how much I carry with me and just pretend I am fine," I clarified. "That's what this place does. Depresses. Represses. Suppresses," she emphasized.

People like me were hardly represented in any subject.[2] U.S. History, heck even Texas History, did not account for non-Anglo perspectives of colonization. The *Maldonado Miracle* was the only novel I remember reading for a class that did not center white characters. It was still written by white man though. It wasn't until my senior year in high school when we read *A Raisin in the Sun.* The essays I had to write had to be written in English. The vocabulary words I had to learn were English words. Of course, until my high school's *foreign* language requirement, which was way too basic and boring for me, but even that was still at odds with me. In my family, *zacate* means grass, and we use the word *guajolote* for turkey, and the vosotros form is totally useless and insignificant. Many of our Spanish words, like those above, are of Nahuatl origin. It is a Spanish that resulted directly from the Spanish colonization of what we now know as Latin America and most of the U.S. Southwest. In academic settings, it is not considered the *right* kind of Spanish.

My friends did not know Spanish. The few other Mexican/Mexican-American students didn't speak Spanish at school. Some of them seemed to even hide the fact that they spoke it at all, especially in our *foreign* language Spanish classes. Even I did. Once, a white guy in my

---

2. I saw myself ALWAYS represented and centered in my school curriculum. Now, I'm sure that I most often saw white MEN holding positions of power relative to white women, but white women were always there, supporting the efforts of "civilization," of "progress" (aka, colonization and white supremacy) even if in a helpmate kind of role (see Newman, 1999). I can't even fathom the depth of the ways that shaped my ability to see myself in the world. And the depth with which it shaped a social psychopathology (Matias, 2016) of always needing to BE the center, be centered. Otherwise, who am I? This is a REAL question I think we all need to ask ourselves as white folks: *Who are we if we are not the center, colonizing, dominating, white? Who are we if we divest from our attachments to white supremacy? What work would we be doing? Who would we be living with and loving? What would we be writing, how, and with whom? What would we have given up? And what emotional, psychological, and intellectual resources would it have taken for us to get there?*

Spanish class randomly told me he thought this white girl in class was smarter than me because she was having to learn the language to make good grades, but I already knew it. I guess the fact that I was a *homegrown* bilingual excludes me from being considered intelligent. Guess my grades in Spanish classes didn't let me hide it as much as I should have in order to not make white people get in their feelings[3] about it. I would purposefully get some answers wrong to keep my grades at a low A. As time went on and I spent more time in predominantly white spaces, and around predominantly white people, the less I spoke Spanish at home. It didn't seem to be much of an issue since we (my immediate family) were all bilingual.

February 2018. My last grandparent died. My paternal grandmother. According to my aunt by marriage, my grandma had requested a bilingual funeral. As one of her three biological granddaughters, at her mass, I was asked to read. We (the three granddaughters) had done this a decade ago at my paternal grandfather's funeral as well. This time, I hesitated to agree. In an attempt to interpret my hesitancy, my aunt said, "Don't worry. You can read one of the ones in English." I replied, "It doesn't matter." I didn't hesitate because I was worried about reading and speaking in Spanish. I hesitated because I lean towards atheism.

Like the Spanish my family speaks, the prevalence of Catholicism in Latin America and its continual acceptance in Mexican-American homes is not only a result of but is also modern-day colonization. Spanish colonizers used religion as a way to delegitimize and extinguish Indigenous languages, practices, transition, beliefs, knowledge, and people. However, like the Spanish we speak, the Catholicism we practice

---

3. This "white people getting in their feelings" hits home for me. I know those feelings intimately and can smell them when they crop in white people around me, or in myself. White people—white women especially—expect People of Color to make us feel comfortable, to respond to our (micro)aggressions with "niceness," and to take care of us emotionally, as well as materially (Ozias, 2017). The landscape of white feelings is narcissistic; we constantly re-center whiteness through feelings of guilt, helplessness in the form of "performance(s) of racial ignorance that relinquish racial culpability," and self-victimization (Matias, 2016, p.70). A recovery process from the social psychopathology of whiteness (Matias, 2016) requires deep emotional work and constant lifelong vigilance against the ways that whiteness constantly sneaks in, or ambushes (Yancy, 2008). Cheryl Matias's (2016) and Barbara Applebaum's (2010) work are both good places to start. But women of color (in addition to Cheryl Matias) have been naming and explaining the emotional violence that white women do to women and communities of color for decades, even centuries. (See Collins, 2002; Moraga and Anzaldua, 1983; Lorde, 1984; Wells, 1900.)

also does not exist without embedded Indigenous influences. I see and hear traces of culture and traditions that survived the Spanish conquistadores. It doesn't end there though. Remember the Alamo? Peoples had to be colonized twice for me to exist as I am today. So, I let white Jesus go as I started to work to peel off as much colonization as I can, knowing full and well that it cannot end with fighting for SRTOL, the illegitimate Spanish I know. But, it's a start.

"Switching codes is more complex than people think. It doesn't mean your Spanish is bad," said my prof in the one semester of the heritage-track Spanish class I was enrolled in as an undergrad. He was Puertorriqueño. He had originally planned that the students in his SPAN 1301 class would only speak Spanish. We. all. refused. At a Hispanic (Counting?) Serving Institution in South Texas. Day in and day out, I could see he tried to get us to embrace our heritage language, to validate and help us strengthen and believe in our connection to the language formal education taught us to neglect. He cared. SPAN 1302, the next heritage-track Spanish course, didn't make the following semester. Not enough students signed up. I had to enroll in and complete three non-heritage track Spanish classes for my degree requirements. Three easy but extremely boring A's on my transcript. Overall, all of my education up until this SPAN 1301 class refused to accept me as a knower, as someone who wields more than English as a language, as someone who makes meaning in two different languages as well as in a mixture of the two. My education also refused to see the importance of that. As a result, I never tried to test out of Spanish classes because I had already internalized that I didn't know the right kind of Spanish well enough. Failing would have made me feel like more of a fraud—Spanglish, worse: Tex-Mex Spanglish.

I waited for her to walk away before I looked. It was an A+. I don't remember saying anything in response. I probably just faked a smile. After all, I had made the whole thing up. I was 11 and I knew what a waste it would be to take the time out of my mom's day to ask her about my first words and first steps. I guess I only felt guilty, like I had cheated, when my sixth grade English teacher said to me, "I didn't expect that you would write so well!" But, whatever I felt, it wasn't affirmation and it wasn't happiness. Her *compliment* didn't make me feel good. I was always a good student, good at school, but apparently I was not supposed to be.

This teacher made an assumption of me, a racist one. There is no such thing as a racist compliment. It's just racist.[4]

Surprisingly—and yes, I mean surprisingly because by this point, despite all evidence to the contrary, after being told time and time again that I was neither the expected nor desired—I was good enough at school and writing to make it into a PhD program. It still doesn't feel good. My first semester in college, when my first-year composition instructor required us to go to the learning center to have a writing tutor check over our papers and staple The Signed Slip to our essays, it didn't feel good. When I sat at the table across the writing tutor as an undergrad, shaking, heart racing, on the verge of tossing my cookies, it did not feel good. Being under the eye of a deficit perspective does not feel good.

After I shared my story of identity loss because of English-Only policies and a white woman I admire and look up to responded with "Well, I can also see the other side, since they are coming here," it did not feel good. When I questioned the helpfulness of a professor's comments in order to negotiate for feedback I could find helpful and was told that "reviewer feedback is a gift": *sigh*.

When I am thanked by white women for the opportunity to learn from me, from my resistance, struggle, mi testimonio, my life as an undead graduate student, it does not feel good. It does not feel good because under their cheerful, enthusiastic appreciation, there does not seem to be an awareness of how much it costs me that they are STILL having to learn.[5] Lastly, recognizing that it has taken way too long for

4. I am sitting, heavy and unsettled, by this aggression disguised as affirmation. I want to think I've never done this, but I am sure I have. As a well-meaning (and damage doing) white writing consultant/tutor, I wanted to embrace a focus on writers' strengths. Instead I revealed my racist assumptions about writers of color. As a writing center administrator, I do this anytime I believe a white faculty member over a student of color when the authenticity of the student's writing is questioned. Or when I assume the Latina consultants on the writing center staff will all be friends or share common schooling and home culture experiences. Sue et al. (2007) call these microaggressions, specifically microinvalidations. The effect for writers and writing center staff of color is not just psychological and intellectual (epistemologically violent), but also physical. It can result in racial battle fatigue, characterized by high blood pressure, anxiety, depression, and other chronic health and mental health issues (Franklin, Smith, and Hung, 2014; Soto, Dawson-Andoh, and BeLue, 2011). All because white women like myself do not work hard enough to check our racist assumptions and engage in racial healing. It is epistemological violence that has not only psychological but also physical effects.

5. When I read Anna's testimonio, I want to separate myself from the white women she describes. I think, "I would never!" But I *am* those white women. If you are white,

me to write this as a Xicana does not feel good at all. I wonder if I had written it earlier, if I had been encouraged to question my relationship to education, to see the importance and value of my experience, if I wouldn't have lost so much?

———————————

When I began to write this I wondered, "where does one story truly begin or end?" And I thought, "If this is a composite counterstory set in a university writing center, then should it start with a (Ch)Xicana in her first year of college?" Who am I kidding? I know what I have been taught as an academic. I knew how I was expected to begin, to write a composite story because it includes data and isn't just a subjective, anecdotal account. So, in the months between deciding to co-author this piece and writing this piece, I was stuck. Moira and I had met a handful of times, started multiple Google Docs with notes and ideas we developed during our meetings, but nothing. I. Could. Not. Even. At any rate, our original intention was to write a composite counterstory of a (Ch)Xicana writing center

———————————

you are those white women, too. So I ask you, white readers, and myself: *How might we learn to listen if we gave up the need to feel like and be seen as good Whites?* (Thompson, 2003, p. 21). What happens when we start from the place of knowing we're always already complicit in white violence and colonization? Mariana Ortega (2006) calls the good intentions of well-meaning white women "lovingly, knowingly ignorant." And sometimes just arrogantly ignorant. Some white women give zero fucks about People of Color and police the boundaries of the academy loyally and without hesitation. Many more white women—especially those of us who find ourselves wanting to "help" in writing centers and voicing commitments to social justice—continue to erase, silence, and marginalize people and communities of color through our "loving, knowing ignorance." I wonder how many of us sit for long periods of time in the place of *not knowing* (Mayo, 2004), of *checking* ourselves and taking ALL the seats (Ortega, 2006), of releasing control (of spaces, of language, of bodies, of budgets, of policies and procedures) and the material, psychological, and emotional benefits that come with control (Matias, 2016; Harris, 1993)? How many of us start our ways of living, being, teaching, and learning from the place that recognizes our complicity in white supremacy, white violence, and white domination? This is where white women and writing centers must begin. So that instead of saying "thank you" every time we learn something at the expense of a person of color, instead of insisting that oppressive habits and traditions are "gifts," we say that was my fault and risk the privileges and advantages we have to name and resist whiteness, being an active race traitor (Ignatiev, 1997, p. 613). As Lugones and Spelman (1990) tell us:

> You need to learn to become unintrusive, unimportant, patient to the point of tears, while at the same time open to learning any possible lessons. You will also have to come to terms with the sense of alienation, of not belonging, of having your world thoroughly disrupted, having it criticized and scrutinized from the point of view of those who have been harmed by it, having important concepts central to it dismissed, being viewed with mistrust, being seen as of no consequence except as an object of mistrust. (Lugones & Spelman, 1990, p. 31)

which took into consideration the many, differing needs of (Ch)Xicana writers beyond the struggle for life-affirming humanization. As is evident, it wasn't the story that was meant to be written or shared.

Ultimately, I will not feign to know why or pretend there was one solid reason my story took the spotlight and why it took the shape it did. Maybe it was ethereal inspiration, a subconscious attempt to heal, to realign my mind-body-spirit, to accept what the academy rejects day in and day out. Whatever it was, I do feel Moragas's words resonate: "Just as Chicana and other border tongues are de-legitimized, so is the embodiment of that discourse. But it is the author's body that is the constant reminder that knowledge 'fully saturated with history and social life' (Harding, 1991) is a possibility, a knowledge that refuses to be 'kept down'" (as quoted in Cruz, 2001, p. 658). Thus, in this piece, I work to reject the dominating social life and history of academic knowledge, and to bring out, embody, and legitimize my Xicana social life, history, and its knowledge.

As I wrote, I also wondered about our understanding of and desire to situate our intended counterstory beyond the struggle for life-affirming humanization. While we understood how idealistic and maybe even over-ambitious it was to envision (Ch)Xicana beyond the white gaze/ free of white superiority, I didn't realize until writing that in daily life, life-affirming humanization is a continual need and process. Does whiteness result from lack of need to do so? I also worried that in my telling I was denying this process to my parents, whom I see as the other two critical people in my story and are important to consider when thinking of a (Ch)Xicana writing center.

But as I continued to remember and write, what became clear to me as I wrote was that this story isn't just about me. It's about the ways in which white supremacy enacts violence on entire families and thus communities. The very process of including them is in part my attempt to push back against master narratives which perpetuate the myths of meritocracy, individuality, and racist beliefs that Mexican-Americans do not value education and cannot live up to their white counterparts in the classroom—all while by employing some twisted, gaslighting *logic* of objectivity.

"He loved you all. But it really hurt him that no one ever gave him a chance," my aunt (my dad's older sister) said to me after his burial. I didn't have to ask for clarification. I knew she meant in terms of degree-equivalent work, why he was the one of his siblings that "didn't make it." Even with an associate's degree—an opportunity that his gender and regional socio-economic class in the Borderlands enabled for him, he still worked jobs most of his life that didn't require much if any education at all. As I suggested earlier, my father's identity development, although he was closer in proximity to whiteness because of his class, kept him from being white enough to succeed outside of the U.S. Borderlands.

Interconnectedly, my mother didn't "make it" (succeed according to white standards) simply because she supposedly wasn't smart enough or good enough at school, at least that's the narrative she internalized and attested to. While my mother's ethnicity, gender, class, and sexuality shaped her path, institutional racism has shaped the South Texas Borderlands and all the lives who rely on the resources within geographic reach. For my mom those resources were education, land, and family. The latter two were the ones to which she had more access. For my immediate family and my mother's family, seasonal migrant work was one resource afforded to us all, and it allowed us to tap into and replenish another resource: family. We labored together. Aunts. Uncles. Cousins. Brothers. Sisters. Parents. Husbands. Wives. Children. And family friends.

I am quite aware of the fact that I have presented a somewhat romanticized version of seasonal migrant work. Trust when I say that I know it is hard work because I experienced it firsthand. Waking up in the early hours of the day, before the sun was even out. Picking out clothes to protect my body from nature—bugs and the sun—and also from human-made pesticides. Developing calluses from carrying and swinging the azadón into the ground. Working through the soreness and aches. The sweat and thirst in the Texas heat. The romanticized memories exist beside those facts because it is a time I see myself strongly connected to my family. I look back at that time with envy, because I see had characteristics of Xicana identity I wish I never lost and still had today. I see it as a time in my life when Spanish was my first language, when I was more defined by Spanish-Mexican colonial whiteness than British-U.S. colonial whiteness. Let me put it this way, thanks to (but not sincerely though) Mexico's independence from Spain, then Texas's war for independence, followed by the Mexican-American war, my immediate family and my mother's side of the family identified as Mexican in relation to U.S. whiteness. Not that one kind of colonization is better than the other, but they do affect me in different ways—the idea of mestizaje in the U.S. versus in Latin America, the politics of the "X" in Xicana. In the U.S., British colonialism controls the dominant narrative, which positions its presence and domination as rightful and destined, a narrative that most formal education begins to instill into children in the country at the youngest possible age. Who would I be today if I hadn't let that education erase pieces of me?

As I came to value education not only for my love of learning, but also as my way out of poverty, I lacked criticalness. Education was education. I needed it to be successful. And I was good at school. I never asked why English was for school and Spanish was for home, why I was only allowed to learn and demonstrate knowing in one language. I never asked where people like me fit into history or literature or science. It is what it is. At the end of the day it makes sense that if the language I saw as connected to my racialized ethnic identity wasn't represented in formal education, why would I expect to learn about people like me in classes? Without ever having representation, how would I know what I didn't have? Without knowledge of Mexican-American civil rights, especially in education, how would I have known that it wasn't just people who were racist but the whole actual system?

"Anna, if it's all so racist, how did you get this far?"

Unlike my parents:

- I don't "speak with an accent"—at least not anymore—or as during my PhD program a white woman faculty member once declared after asking me if I speak Spanish and I confirmed with a yes, "you must be hiding it"
- I learned to enact whiteness because I was taught by primarily white women teachers
- I attended schools in small predominantly white towns with small class sizes, which led me to have "college ready" grades before attending a MSI-HSI for my bachelor's and master's degree—although my ACT and GRE scores weren't that great
- I gained white women mentors at the MSI-HSI I attended who without a doubt helped me get accepted into a predominantly white R1 university
- I've been given the chance to attend a predominantly white R1 university presumably as the token minority—the other PhD students admitted at the same time were white
- I ended up halfway disconnected from my family, culture, and history via the valuing of Eurocentric education that upholds white supremacy
- I realized I ended up halfway disconnected from my family, culture, and history via the valuing of Eurocentric education that upholds white supremacy and am in recovery. I'm sure that is a continual, lifelong process for people like me.

Given the memories and details I have shared up to this point, would a university writing center be enough for me, my mother, and/or my father? I am not convinced. Would a (Ch)Xicana university writing center be enough for me, my mother, and/or my father? Yet again, I am not convinced. Why? Because of the colonial impulses of the academy. One example of such an impulse is its deficit perspective of People of Color that it continues to reproduce. Another example of such a colonial impulse is the need to generalize and universalize experiences, which is a problem because of, as I hope my narrative highlights, the way even just three immediate family members living in the same household can be affected in different but related ways by white supremacy.[6]

One thing I do believe is the need to move away from centering the act of *academic* writing because in its current, common iteration, "training racially minoritized writers to center a white audience" (Treviño, 2018a) is one of the outcomes, which "helps keep white supremacy in place by making sure white people are seen as the only ones with power, authority, and agency" (Treviño, 2018a). Instead, we Xicanas "need to teach, learn, and be with writing in ways that work for us . . ." (Treviño, 2018a), ways that allow us "to consider our rhetorical ability to read our experiences alongside others and to connect as a strategy for survival" (Leon, 2010, p. 23). These connections should span across and beyond institutions. Establishing such connections requires us to push against, out, and disperse. Instead of working to recreate writing centers, we need writing coalitions to counter the prevalence of hegemonic feminism in the field of writing studies and the way we think, teach, and learn about writing.

REFERENCES

Applebaum, B. (2010). *Being White, Being Good: White Complicity, White Moral Responsibility, and Social Justice Pedagogy*. Lexington Books.

Battiste, M. (2013). *Decolonizing Education: Nourishing the Learning Spirit*. Purich Publishing Limited.

BlackPast, B. (2010, July 13). (1900) Ida B. Wells, "Lynch Law in America." https://www.blackpast.org/african-american-history/1900-ida-b-wells-lynch-law-america/

Collins, P. H. (2002). *Black Feminist Thought: Knowledge, Consciousness, and the Politics of Empowerment*. Routledge.

Cruz, C. (2001). Toward an epistemology of a Brown body. *International Journal of Qualitative Studies in Education, 14*(5), 657–669. https://doi.org/10.1080/09518390110059874

Elenes, C. A. (2000). Chicana feminist narratives and the politics of the self. *Frontiers: A Journal of Women Studies, 21*(3), 105–123. http://www.jstor.org/stable/3347113

Franklin, J. D., Smith, W. A., & Hung, M. (2014). Racial battle fatigue for Latina/o students: A quantitative perspective. *Journal of Hispanic Higher Education, 13*(4), 303–322. https://doi.org/10.1177/1538192714540530

---

6. P.S. By now I am sure you are wondering about the fotos mentioned in the subtitle. In the original drafts, I included photographs alongside my memories. At the end, I thought about whom I intended to be the primary audience for my narrative and whom I intended to be the secondary audience. I still felt uncomfortable, so I've done as Carrillo suggested in *This Bridge Called My Back*: taken them with me. However, I didn't want to change the subtitle because it is a reference to a Selena song. People like me may have not been represented in school, I may have lost parts of myself to whiteness, but I've always had Selena, y yo siempre tendrá mis fotos conmigo.

Harris, C. I. (1993). Whiteness as property. *Harvard Law Review, 106*(8), 1707–1791. https://doi.org/10.2307/1341787

Ignatiev, N. (1997). How to be a race traitor: Six ways to fight being white. In R. Delgado & J. Stefancic (Eds.), *Critical White Studies: Looking Behind the Mirror* (p. 613). Temple University Press.

Leon, K. M. (2010). Building a Chicana rhetoric for rhetoric and composition [Doctoral dissertation, Michigan State University]. MSU Libraries Digital Repositories. https://doi.org/10.25335/M5SN0146V

Lorde, A. (1984). *Sister Outsider: Essays and Speeches.* Crossing Press.

Lugones, M. C., Spelman, E. V., Lugones, M. C., & Spelman, E. V. (1983). Have we got a theory for you! Feminist theory, cultural imperialism and the demand for 'the woman's voice.' *Women's Studies International Forum, 6*(6), 573–581. https://doi.org/10.1016/0277-5395(83)90019-5

Matias, C. E. (2016). *Feeling White: Whiteness, Emotionality, and Education.* Sense Publishers.

Mayo, C. (2004). Certain privilege: Rethinking white agency. *Philosophy of Education Archive,* 308–316.

Moraga, C., & Anzaldúa, G. (Eds.). (1983). *This Bridge Called My Back: Radical Writings by Women of Color.* Kitchen Table.

Newman, L. M. (1999). *White Women's Rights: The Racial Origins of Feminism in the United States.* Oxford University Press.

Nicolazzo, Z. (2016). *Trans* in College: Transgender Students' Strategies for Navigating Campus Life and the Institutional Politics of Inclusion.* Stylus Publishing.

Ortega, M. (2006). Being lovingly, knowingly ignorant: White feminism and women of color. *Hypatia, 21*(3), 56–74. https://doi.org/10.1111/j.1527-2001.2006.tb01113.x

Ozias, M. (2017). White women doing racism: A critical narrative inquiry of white women's experiences of college [Doctoral dissertation, University of Oklahoma]. ShareOK. https://shareok.org/handle/11244/51916

Soto, J. A., Dawson-Andoh, N. A., & BeLue, R. (2011). The relationship between perceived discrimination and generalized anxiety disorder among African Americans, Afro Caribbeans, and non-Hispanic whites. *Journal of Anxiety Disorders, 25*(2), 258–265. https://doi.org/10.1016/j.janxdis.2010.09.011

Spade, D. (2011). *Normal Life: Administrative Violence, Critical Trans Politics, and the Limits of Law.* South End Press.

Sue, D. W., Capodilupo, C. M., Torino, G. C., Bucceri, J. M., Holder, A. M. B., Nadal, K. L., & Esquilin, M. (2007). Racial microaggressions in everyday life: Implications for clinical practice. *American Psychologist, 62*(4), 271–286. https://doi.org/10.1037/0003-066X.62.4.271

Thompson, A. (2003). Tiffany, Friend of people of color: White investments in antiracism. *International Journal of Qualitative Studies in Education, 16*(1), 7–29. https://doi.org/10.1080/0951839032000033509

Treviño, A. [@aktrevi]. (2018a, December 3). Still thinking through this. I'm really trying to de-center the idea of the default audience being white and middle class, especially in writing classes so that students can use and develop their entire non-appropriative linguistic repertoires, because I think. [Tweet].twitter.com/aktrevi/status/1069613862385827840.

Treviño, A. [@aktrevi]. (2018b, November 3). WOC need use, teach, learn, and be with writing in ways that work for us. Centering the act of centering isn't enough. We need "to consider our rhetorical ability to read our expenses alongside others and to connect . . ." [Tweet]. twitter.com/aktrevi/status/1058786913589624832.

Yancy, G. (2008). *Black Bodies, White Gazes: The Continuing Significance of Race.* Rowman & Littlefield Publishers.

SECTION TWO

CounterStories from the Writing Center

5

THE STORIES WE TELL AND DON'T TELL IN THE WRITING CENTER

Romeo García and Douglas S. Kern

The writing center community (WCC) continues to bear witness to an anti-racist and social justice turn, though not all are responsive to it. This turn, it must be noted, has roots in earlier writing center (WC) work, in which scholars labored to illustrate how WCs are overdetermined by a history that is colonial, ideological, and hierarchal (see Lunsford, 1991; Grimm, 1996a/1996b/1999; Bawarshi & Pelkowski, 1999; Barron & Grimm, 2002). Will there ever have been a time, in the past or the present, to think of the writing center as anything but a wound(ed/ing) place (see Till, 2012; Brasher et al., 2017)? We continue to wonder. The turn also has roots in the 2005 National Conference on Peer Tutoring in Writing. Victor Villanueva (2006) was the keynote and gave a talk that would be published as "Blind: Talking about the new racism." There, he implicates the WCC, he indicts us, tells us not to be blind to "what we know is still racism" (p. 18). Will there ever have been a time, in the past or the present, to justify the neglect of racism and a WC's complicity with it? Since then, the WCC has contemplated how "racism" has been sold to them rhetorically, how they have purchased it, and how the business of managing and controlling the circulation and flow of bodies evidences the material reality of racism (see Davila, 2006; Weaver, 2006; Bennet, 2008; DeCiccio, 2012; Diab et al., 2012; Dees et al., 2007; Geller et al., 2007/2011; Greenfield and Rowan, 2011; Ozias & Godbee, 2011; Zhang et al., 2013). No degree of progress can ever dismiss the number of students and tutors of color who have been subjugated under a determined concept of benevolent progress that supposes the singularity of a presentation and representation of being and a teleological explication of the WC. The anti-racist and social justice turn owes much to past scholarship. Its formal inauguration, however, can be traced to a seminal piece in the WCC.

One of the earliest pieces of scholarship that calls WCs to undertake anti-racist work is Frankie Condon's (2007) article, "Beyond the

https://doi.org/10.7330/9781646421534.c005

known: Writing centers and the work of anti-racism." There, she implicates white WC directors and tutors who work at Predominantly White Institutions (PWIs) to take on racism. Condon writes, "To take on racism is, in a critical sense, to take on ourselves; to struggle not only to re-make our world, but also to remake our consciousness" (p. 30). Her work inspired WCs to be attentive to their mission statements, policies, and practices; to see anti-racist work as the human work WCs do (also see Draxler, 2007). Such can be evidenced in Laura Greenfield and Karen Rowan's edited collection, *Writing Centers and the New Racism.* Within that collection, Moira Ozias and Beth Godbee's (2011) "Organizing for anti-racism in writing centers" reminds the WCC that anti-racist and organizing work must be attentive to local and institutional culture (p. 151). They write, "we must dig deeper to understand how organizing arranges our lives in ways that, when unreflected, can support the status quo, but when intentional and thoughtful, can also work against oppressive structures" (p. 154). Ozias and Godbee (2011) seek a WC and WCC that is transformed.

Condon's work can also be seen in Rasha Diab, Beth Godbee, Thomas Ferrel, and Neil Simpkins' (2012) collaborative work in "A multidimensional pedagogy for racial justice in writing centers." Here is one of the first instances of bringing together anti-racist and social justice work more explicitly. Arguing anti-racist and social justice work should be more than a "statement" (p. 1), they write, "Because writing centers are literacy and language sites . . . a pedagogy for racial justice in writing centers operates through all aspects of our work" (p. 3). Thus, because "racism is both structural and everyday," Diab et al. (2012) explain, "anti-racism too must be structural and everyday" (p. 6). Their pedagogy for racial justice, hence, is multidimensional: processual and reiterative, reflective and attentive, and embodied and engaged. In all, Diab et al. (2012) bring together an agenda that strives to work towards equity and racial justice that begins with questioning the following: "what we know (knowledge), how we know (our lived experience and methods), how we position ourselves in relation to others (stances), and how we think and act in the world everyday (actions)" (p. 6). This agenda, more importantly, is undertaken with the goal of re-making the WC space as a site of anti-racist and social justice work (also see Arao & Clemens, 2013). At the heart of this work is questioning a certain primordial value of WC work.

One recent example of the materialization of anti-racist and social justice work is the statement/document put out by the WC at the University of Washington-Tacoma (UWT). This statement, their website says, "informs our center's practices and on-going assessment efforts to improve our practices" (n.p.). Within the document, which is compartmentalized into "Our Beliefs" and "Our Commitment," the UWT WC refers to our society as racist. The document reads as follows: "Racism is the normal condition of things. Racism is pervasive. It is in the systems, structures, rules, languages, expectations, and guidelines that make up our classes, school, and society" (n.p.). Will there ever have been a time, in the past or the present, to think of the WC as anything but a microcosmic reproduction of that society: power structures, power differentials, human capital? The document addresses how the WCC there sees their work, as members who are responsible, as Villanueva (2006) stated in his keynote, of teaching the art of conversation. Here, the art of conversation involves critical reflection, awareness and critique of racism and oppressive structures that bear down upon all. The "all" is significant here, for even those who do not "intentionally" perpetuate racism or social injustices are still entangled and complicit in a racist society. For the WCC there, anti-racist and social justice practices means a commitment to humanity where it is not yet. The anti-racist and social justice turn has indeed proven to be a necessary intervention into value systems that enable a certain primordial value of WC work to preserve.

We, the co-authors here, hate to be the contrarian figures. But as we celebrate the anti-racist and social justice turn, it is important to not do so in excess. Among every story we tell of anti-racist and social justice commitments, there are countless stories entangled and/or complicit in racism and social injustices. Thus, it is important to beware a turn that keeps the same rhetorical spine: a turn (a *polis*) that carves itself out as a commonplace (*topoi*), a site that produces work predicated on a central belief (*doxa*)—to serve the common good (phronesis)—, work that is still linked to a diseased nervous system (e.g., a certain type of metaphysics). Toward these ends, to echo Nancy Grimm, we are not sure WC work accomplishes as much as it is thought to do with regard to the anti-racist and social justice turn. It is important to remember that while every turn that occurs, inside and outside of the WC, is obviously made under certain conditions, not every person will be on board. WCs are sites of power, relations of power, which can only be understood through an analysis of actions and motives; we must ask, how much of white benevolence is a reproduction of desire, of power, of a constellation capable of elaborating the myth of progress. Our guess is that there will remain those committed to an anti-racist and social justice turn and those invested in preserving hierarchy in the name of the WC serving the common good.

In particular, however, we're concerned, as with the other chapters in this book, with the WC's overdetermined colonial, ideological, and hierarchical histories, as well the presence (and preservation) of white benevolence. Behind white benevolence there is a deceptive "well-meaningness" that actually works to undo any real politics or potential regarding anti-racism and social justice. This calls our attention to thoughtful questions expressed in two separate articles: (1) how can anti-racist commitments become manifest and actionable (Diab et al., 2012) and (2) how do we mitigate the conflict between WC best practices and the experiences of People of Color (Condon, 2009)? It is from such questions that we submit here stories of white benevolence. In what follows, we account for stories we tell and stories we don't tell that paint a striking image of this concept of deceptive benevolence and the work still left to be done. Specifically, we focus on the rhetoric and discourse of "We Do/We Don't Have That Problem Here." We reflect on the kind of emotional labor placed upon People of Color who are both constantly resisting tokenization and having to "speak up."

Will there ever have been a time, in the past or the present, to think an anti-racist and social justice turn without our white benevolent agents?

WE DO HAVE THAT PROBLEM HERE

Over the years, I've (Romeo) had many conversations with WC consultants and directors. The majority of them, I must say, are white. (There is nothing inherently wrong with the fact that they are white. My first WC mentor is white.) Many of our conversations focus on anti-racist and social justice work. And, being the contrarian person that I am, I strive to redirect the conversation to the limits of this work, to the overdetermination of this work expressed in terms of certainty. Of course, this is not always met with gratitude. Nonetheless, the takeaway, on both ends, is beneficial. I for one leave those conversations wondering the following: What does the WC mean by anti-racist and social justice work? Is there a disconnect between what WCs say they are doing and how they are actually carrying out the work? And how does white benevolence, both as a historical problem and a possible resolution for the WC, ensure that the WC is written and rewritten as colonial, ideological, and hierarchical (e.g., a wound[ed/ing] place)? These questions lead me to think about all kinds of scenarios, including one in which a white benevolent WC director acknowledged, "We have that [racism and injustices] problem here!" In what follows, I play out this scenario across three scenes, according to conversations I've had in the past. Overall, my words of caution are that anti-racist and social justice agendas have the potential to induce white pleasure and white desire. I conclude my section with some recommendations.

A SETTING

The WC director is white; born and raised in a white community, educated at a PWI, and working now at a similar PWI. This director has never had to come to terms with their whiteness; that is their privilege. There has been no need to because both the city and school in which they work is predominantly white. Anti-racist and social justice agendas are out of sight and out of mind. Those kinds of projects are typically meant for institutions with People of Color. The director educates consultants under the auspices of business as usual. But changes are on the horizon. The administration tells faculty they must prepare for demographic changes at their campus. This worries the director. A feeling of inadequacy sets in. They begin to read up on Western history: colonization, oppression, and white supremacy. This saddens the director. So, they turn to the listservs as they begin to undertake and seek to embody a social justice warrior ethos. Changes come faster than expected, with more students of color than anticipated. The WC director struggles for the first four years, especially with a culture on campus that reveals racist tendencies. "We have that problem here," the director acknowledges. They will spend the next four years designing policies, best practices, and training informed by anti-racist and social justice agendas.

In the fifth year, things are going well at the WC. The campus, however, continues to prove that there is a racist problem. This reality remains the impetus for the white director to implement anti-racist and social justice agendas. The shelves are stocked with books by authors of color. The walls display anti-racist and social justice mottos and statements. All consultants undergo training with anti-racist and social justice philosophies informing their experience. The director is still unsatisfied. The WC remains predominantly white. It does not reflect the dynamic student demographics of the university. "How can the writing center not be another white space?" the director contemplates. They set three goals to ensure that the writing center becomes a safe space: (1) hire consultants, administrators, and staff from diverse backgrounds, (2) continue to read, talk, and write about racism and social injustices during training, and (3) engage faculty members in and around topics of anti-racism and social injustices. A safe and diverse space the writing center will be, as the director continues with seeing the goals through.

SCENARIO #1: HIRING PRACTICES

The white writing center director acknowledges, "We have that problem here." They have observed it. They have been part of the systematic and pervasive infrastructure of racism and social injustices. Now, they want to disentangle themselves from that structure, for they imagine a writing center that can be, in practice and theory, a site of anti-racism and social justice. As a writing center director, they see an opportunity to foster such an environment. For them, it begins with hiring practices. They contemplate. "I can hire someone to work with strictly Spanish-speaking students." They continue to contemplate further, imagining a writing center with diverse bodies. "I need particular bodies as consultants, so they can see we are diverse." They pull particular names from the pool of applications and begin making rounds of inquiry into whether or not those students are still interested in being consultants. The director schedules one as soon as that Friday. They are both excited.

Friday comes around. The Brown(ed) student is sitting on the couches waiting to be interviewed. The student is greeted not by the writing center director, but by the student-secretary at the front, despite the director seeing them. 1 minute has passed. 2 minutes have passed . . . 3, 4, and then 5 minutes. The white writing center director emerges from their chair to greet the potential candidate. The student wonders why the director is 5 minutes late. The white writing center director has no reason other than they lost track of time. But, time matters, especially in an interview, especially for a student, whose very presence in such a place is a precarious one.

"Thank you for coming in," the white writing center director states to the student. The student is still a little sour from the fact that they had to wait longer than necessary. Moreover, they were not even greeted by the writing center director who saw them. "You are welcome," the student responds to the director. "Shall we start?" the director asks. The student is confident and strong; they know their worth at the same time they know what it means to be in a wound(ed/ing) place. "I can see you working with Spanish-speaking students," the director states as they go over their vision for why they might possibly hire the student. This puzzles the student and leads the student to respond, "And I can work with other students because I know English besides Spanish." This response seems to not phase the director and they follow it up with, "Yes, I know you know English, but Spanish-speaking students will be happy to know they can work with someone like them." This statement further puzzles the student. The student knows what this is—they are being tokenized. "I cannot and will not be a token," the student affirms strongly to the director.

The white writing center director finishes their hiring of diverse bodies to show the university a commitment to students of color. We will never know, however, how many students felt tokenized during the interview process; we will never know how many students arrived only that they will never have arrived. The director's acknowledgement of "We have that problem here" is overshadowed and undercut by her rhetoric of tokenization. Good intentions do not always equivocate to anti-racism and social justice discourse. Good intentions sometimes are entangled and/or complicit too in white ignorance and white arrogance. And, on top of that, the director was only able to hire two students of color out of the twelve consultants they hired overall.

SCENARIO #2: READING, TALKING, AND WRITING ABOUT IT

Not knowing how they made the Brown student feel, the white writing center director continues pursuing an anti-racist and social justice turn. The director plans. "I can talk about racism . . . I can ask consultants to reflect upon their experiences with racism." The director contemplates. "That is social justice, right?" The director continues to plan. "I can have students read, talk, and write about racism for the first couple of weeks of training." The director rationalizes. "That is enough anti-racism and social justice work, right?" It is settled. The director and the new consultants will spend a couple of weeks of training focused on anti-racism and social justice. This will make the difference, the director believes.

The first day of training is the same as the first day of classes at the university. Consultants fill the room. The one Brown student gets to the class early, to observe, to listen, to reflect. "Let's see how many People of Color will actually be in this class," the student thinks to themselves. "Let's see how I am further tokenized in these so-called conversations on anti-racism and social justice," the student concerningly thinks, too. The student is optimistic, but doubtful—she has yet to experience a time that proves the contrary. One student walks in—white. Another student walks in—white. Three, four, five, ten students walk in—white. The student finally sees someone—another Brown(ed) student. "Two People of Color. Psh, I knew it," the student says to themselves. "Let's see how this is going to play out."

The white writing center director introduces themselves and welcomes the consultants. The director lays out a vision for anti-racism and social justice work. "We will spend the first two weeks reading, talking, and writing racism," the director states to the consultants. The Brown(ed) student rolls their eyes, not so apparent as to be recognized.

"Two weeks, that's it?" the student thinks to themselves. "Then we will spend the remaining part of your training on writing center pedagogy and theory." There is no explanation though of how this will tie back into anti-racism and social justice work. "Two weeks, really," the Brown student continues to think, as they are bothered by the fact that complex and multifaceted anti-racism and social justice work is being crammed into two weeks. "Will anti-racism and/or social justice ever be more than just an afterthought?"

Week 1: The writing center director spends the first week talking about the history of race in society and collapses the public sphere with the academic and institutional sphere. The director has plans. They will ask the class to expand on their readings by talking and writing about their own experiences with racism. "What do you think about racism, would you like to share your experiences?" the director turns to and asks the only consultants of color. "Really lady?" the Brown(ed) consultant thinks. "Come on, I think it will be very beneficial for other consultants to hear," the director persistently continues. "I can't believe this." This time it is more than a thought, the student's frustration is actually articulated in spoken words. "Is there an issue? We all have to participate in the conversation," the director says. "Yes, but you call on the only two People of Color in the class to speak to white consultants about our experiences with racism." The Brown(ed) student feels the pressure not only from the white writing center director, but also from the white consultants who are anxious to hear about a person of color's experience. "If you are not going to participate, I am going to have to ask you to leave," the director states. The Brown(ed) consultant leaves: difference imposed, exposed, and amplified, dismissed and muted. The Brown(ed) student cannot speak or be heard in and on their own terms.

Week 2: The white writing center director welcomes the training class back for their second week. "Remember, participation is mandatory and though we will have difficult conversations involving racism and social injustices, everyone needs to participate," the director states. They look at the Brown(ed) consultant in the process, whether intentionally or unintentionally, we will never know. After a lecture on the interstices of writing centers, post-colonialism, and identity, the director looks at the Brown(ed) consultant of color and asks them what they think. Whether this is intentional or unintentional, we will never know. "I cannot believe this," the Brown(ed) consultant thinks. "Asks them other white folks, please, I am not your token, I am not here to nurture you into forgiveness or provide guidance," the student says to the white director and white consultants, as they stare at the student in anticipation for what they may or may not say. The Brown(ed) student gets up. "You know if you leave you will not be completing the training," the white director states. "That is fine. I appreciate the opportunity to be considered, but as I said to you in the interview, as I will say now before all these white folks, I am not your token. You cannot use me, my identity or subjectivity as the basis for conversation." The Brown(ed) consultant leaves, again. No response could be proffered.

The white writing center director cannot contemplate what went wrong. They acknowledged, "We have that problem here." They tried to hire diverse consultants. "I've even dedicated two weeks to conversations on racism," the director reflects. It is not enough, as some have argued, to treat the writing center as a brave space. Brave, perhaps, for white consultants and writing center directors who, at the expense of marginalizing or alienating a person of color, alas come to terms. Perhaps what is truly meant by "brave space" is a white person coming to terms with their entanglements and complicities in racism and/or social injustices. Brave presumes, and it is People of Color who have to put such presuppositions in check. The WC remains a wound(ed/ing) place.

SCENARIO #3: DIFFICULT CONVERSATIONS: WHAT DO WE MEAN

The white writing center director intends to have a "come to Jesus" moment with the Brown(ed) consultant. The director rationalizes. "I did nothing wrong! They are in the wrong!" The director schedules a meeting and plans. "I am going to tell them, if they cannot engage in these types of conversations, they cannot be a writing center consultant. This is unacceptable!"

The Brown(ed) consultant comes in for the meeting with the white writing center director. "I knew from the beginning you would be a problem," the director states to the Brown(ed) consultant. "Why?" the consultant states, "Because I don't let you tokenize me, because I speak back, because I am unwilling to put up with white people problems?" the consultant continues. Neither of them can believe what was just stated. On the one hand, the director is angered, while on the other hand, the consultant is satisfied that they spoke their mind. "Well, you can't work here if you are not going to participate," the director responds back. The Brown(ed) consultant contemplates, because on the one hand, they need the money, and on the other hand, is money worth sacrificing integrity? The Brown(ed) consultant, thinking they cannot partake in their own dismissal, takes a deep breath and states, "There are many ways to define participation, and just because I refuse to allow you, or those white consultants to tokenize me, does not mean I am not doing the readings or that I am not engaging in the blog posts. I go to class, I listen, but I refuse to be a token." The director gives in and accepts that the Brown(ed) consultant will not speak on such issues, despite their intentions for anti-racist and social justice pedagogical practice.

The white writing center director reaches out to faculty members after the meeting. One faculty member agrees to meet with the director. The conversation begins with, "do you know this student?" and continues with, "I knew they were going to be a problem when. . . ." The faculty member is taken aback. They ask for clarification, they listen, and they respond. "There is still much work for you to do: (1) you cannot tokenize a person of color, (2) anti-racism and social justice can't be approached as a crash-course, something to be accomplished in two weeks, and (3) you should not tell a student you knew they were a problem from the get-go." The white writing center director attempts to respond, "Moreover," but the faculty member interrupts. As the faculty member provides further explication of the three points made, it becomes evident that the white writing center director has become disengaged.

IMPLICATIONS

What seem to be steps in the right direction, that is, steps necessary for transformative change, end up being steps that create a detrimental environment, one that threatens the agency of consultants, on the one hand, and, on the other, calls into question what we actually mean when we say we *do* anti-racist and social justice work. The purpose of these scenarios is to caution celebrations of anti-racist and social justice turns, and to remind writing center scholars of the insufficiency of simply saying we are going to resist or subvert power and *do* anti-racist and social justice work while remaining consubstantial to that power. There can be no bona fide anti-racist and social justice politics with a timeframe in mind for insofar as we are entangled and complicit in power and ideology all we can do is ensure we are constantly *working* toward a more equitable and just writing center.

We must check the "pleasures" and "desires" that emerge from saying we do anti-racist and social justice work. The scenarios are not meant to say we should not do such work, nor are they meant to suggest that white failure is bad. The difference, however, is in the last scenario, when all conversation is cut off because "pleasures" and "desires" override constructive criticism. I recommend one thing: that we find solace with the fact that a condition of possibility is also its condition of impossibility.

We will all fail. There is so much uncertainty, especially in undertaking this work within an institution that continuously rewrites itself as colonial. Anti-racist and social justice initiatives, I would argue, can only ever be temporary points of departure that must be revised and reoriented. Might we learn to be more open to criticism; this is more capacious for the work that must be done.

WE DON'T HAVE THAT PROBLEM HERE

As we commit to consistently serve bona fide anti-racist and social justice politics, then, it's also imperative that we battle and question direct challenges to anti-racist and social justice practices, as well as the inaction which permeates too many writing centers—such inaction that equates to willful ignorance and mindful dismissal of the already established anti-racist and social justice turn. For example, we'd like to question the International Writing Center Association 2018 call for proposals, which suggested "Writing Center work requires . . . understanding the code." What and which code is referenced here, exactly? Whose code? Infiltrating our institutions as accomplices of anti-racism requires writing centers to look beyond restrictive terms and practices set to control and marginalize. Shouldn't writing center tutors, directors, staff, and the writers that visit seek to understand each other's unique *codes* of communication? Shouldn't the teachers teaching within our institutions? Why don't we dissect and reimagine the specific phrasing used within our centers and institutions (such as the singular use of "code" or Standard Written English), in order to "infiltrate" our institutions as accomplices of anti-racism?

Go ahead. Ask around. We fear you'll hear a familiar phrase: "We don't have that problem here." This rhetorical construction is a type of running away from problems that are always already present—a type of neoliberal turning away. In their monograph, *Racism and Racial Equity in Higher Education*, for example, Samuel D. Museus, María C. Ledesma, and Tara L. Parker (2015) note, "neoliberal ideologies intersect with racism, and promote and perpetuate ways of thinking that highlight individual responsibility in creating racial and other social conditions, while reinforcing color-blind ideologies and downplaying the role of racism in bringing about such conditions" (p. 48). And, these six little words reek of this sort of downplaying—this inaction and avoidance. Six words: We. Don't. Have. That. Problem. Here. Who don't? Who's we? Where's here? The writing center? That's a curious title: center. Are we the epicenters of our institutions? We can't be sure about all centers, but our institutions' writing centers serve any undergraduate with any writing, across any discipline, for any purpose, at any stage of the writing process. Many of our writing centers become the spaces where screenplays meet lab reports, grant proposals meet short fiction, resumes meet poetry. So, yeah, we're in the middle of something. We're in the middle of a diverse population of students and writers, voices and accents, rhythms and styles, choices and chances, drafts and submissions.

Still, even as some work to foster and champion such diversity, others speak and embody this notion that's as dangerous as it is fallacious: we don't have that problem here. Once again, we invite you to imagine a particular scenario to help think this through:

SCENARIO #1: I CAN'T SEE/ADDRESS THAT PROBLEM HERE.

During his downtime (while working in the writing center), a tutor of color takes it upon himself to read—as research—Laura Greenfield and Karen Rowan's *Writing Centers and the New Racism: A Call for Sustainable Dialogue and Change*. The tutor is excited by the arguments and articles put forward throughout the collection. In fact, he's so excited, he approaches his white director to share his excitement: "This book is fantastic," the tutor exclaims. He continues, "We should fold some of these readings into our tutor training sessions!"

"What is it?" the director asks.

Eagerly, the tutor hands the book over to his director. She flips through, murmuring phrases found within the chapter titles listed among the contents page: "Rhetorics of Racism," "Advantage Based on Race." Finally, the director looks up toward the tutor and declares, "Yes, but we don't have that problem here."

Of course, there is a distinct problem here and, given this scenario, it's pretty obvious. The director's inability to acknowledge the book's contents—along with the tutor's helpful suggestions—speaks to the very *problem* the tutor was trying to address/combat by sharing what he'd read in the first place. There's an out-of-sight/out-of-mind mentality regarding racism and equality which can and does occur within all of our institutions (and, without doubt, beyond). Let's consider another scenario for just one possible answer as to why these "yes/but" responses proliferate:

SCENARIO #2: I CAN'T HEAR YOU HERE.

It's late May and the writing center is holding its end-of-semester party for consultants and staff. A white assistant director, having also recently read *Writing Centers and the New Racism*, approaches a tutor of color and asks if she feels constricted by the academy's restrictions on language. Confused, the tutor asks for elaboration. The AD furthers his inquiry by asking if she feels she has to hide, limit, or curb her unique forms of communication within the academic institution. He asks, "Have you ever felt silenced within our center?"

After contemplating the AD's inquiry, the tutor looks at him and replies, "You've never heard the real me. You'll never hear the real me."

Now, we're not here to challenge this tutor's palpable sense of danger, or her propensity to mask a side of herself within the academy—that's her right as a student/her right as a writer. But, how do you think she'd respond to that line of thinking: we don't have that problem here? You see, the tutor response displayed within this scenario isn't (merely) a simple hypothetical. This type of emotional pain is repeatedly rationed out to the marginalized, the other. And, as most in the academy understand, even as they attempt to deny or ignore, that "the other" is defined by this sense of neoliberal racism which penetrates our universities, and, by extension, our centers. Extrapolating concepts from Sara Ahmed's (2004) seminal book, *The Cultural Politics of Emotion*, I'd like to suggest that the tutor's reaction is a social response to that sort of emotional pain brought on by exclusion. There the tutor is invited to a celebration while feeling unable to be her true self. James Baldwin's (2015) Black protagonist from *Tell Me How Long the Train's Been Gone*, Leo Proudhammer, exclaims, "The crowd, no doubt, would have described itself as friendly; a fair observation would have been that they were in a holiday mood. But their holidays, were, emphatically, not my holidays" (p. 172). So, how do you reconcile this tutor's answers if you, too, think, with benevolence, "we don't have that problem here?"

You know, maybe folks who think this way are right. Maybe their phrasing just needs a little, what? Revision. 'Cause we don't remember labeling unique *codes* of communication, or diversity and inclusion, or access and equity, as problems. So, maybe folks are right. These concepts ain't problems; they never were. The problem lies in that line of thinking—the "we don't have that problem" line. A thought that falsely equivocates we as *I* and don't as *can't*: I can't. So, "we don't have that problem here" becomes "I can't see that problem here." "I can't address that problem here." "I can't accept your English here." "I can't hear you here."

Yes, we'll say it again, writing centers need to look anew (with a fresh gaze), beyond restrictive terms and practices set to control and marginalize.

A CONVERSATION BETWEEN ROMEO AND DOUG

What is meant by white benevolence?

Garcia: I am constantly thinking of how to nuance frameworks that ground our interactions and exchanges, be it a relational framework of ethics or an ethical whiteness. For the latter, I contemplate whether this is even a possibility. Can a white body learn to re-exist? Nonetheless, when I think about white benevolence, I think about the caricature that is the white writing center director depicted in the scenarios under the section "We Do Have that Problem Here." So often, I have come across, or have experienced personally, such a director, a director who has good intentions, but whose sense of white innocence and articulation of white denial and ignorance reveals how very few times they have actually been held accountable for their rhetoric and actions. What I am suggesting, here, is that at the very least there is a recipe for "making" white benevolence that is entangled in imperialist and global designs for maintaining and reproducing power. Part of such a recipe encompasses the terms innocence, denial, ignorance, arrogance, fragility and silence. Allow me to provide a review of these terms.

Whiteness, White Privilege, and White Comfort: A pathologizing of whiteness as the universal and non-whiteness as the other. Scholars have long pointed to the sophistication of whiteness and white subjectivity: erasure (of whiteness from the re/making of colonial subjectivities), distance ("I am not a racist"), and deflection (race, racism, and oppression are matters of non-white people). White privilege is much more than the "invisible package of unearned assets" or the "invisible weightless knapsack of special provisions" (McIntosh, 1997, p. 291). It is a set of relational practices: propriety and belonging, the emplacement of structures, and the accrual of privilege at the intersection of epistemic standpoints of erasure, distance, ignorance, fragility, and silence. It is about maintaining entitlements (Andersen, Taylor, Logio, p. 424), and it is a normalizing system of unearned advantages and benefits (Wellman, 1993, p. 61, 113; Sue, 2003, p. 7; Kendall, 2012, p. 63) that are clearly observed. White privilege reflects a myriad of advantages and benefits (Delgado and Stefancic, 2012, p. 87) that have everything to do with ability and intentionality within hegemonic systems or institutions (Pulido, p. 467). There is an effort to create distance and to suggest that raced bodies are not significant. I appreciate a passage by Leslie Carr (1997), "White people are acutely color conscious, not color-blind" (p. 154), because it calls attention to the collective privilege embedded in the ability to exercise the idea that one does not see color. When this student talks about equality, they reveal a contradiction between being color-blind and color-conscious, which allows power to remain evasive.

To echo Bonilla-Silva (2001), this is not a "matter of finding good and bad people" but of examining "collective" understanding and representations (p. 137). As Charles Mills (1997) would argue, even though not all white people are signatories, they are nonetheless beneficiaries of this system of institutions of belonging and entitlement (p. 11). This same sentiment is echoed in "White supremacy," wherein Frances Ansley (1997) asserts, "I do not mean to allude only to the self-conscious racism of white supremacist hate groups. I refer instead to . . . relations of white dominance and non-white subordination . . . daily reenacted across a broad array of institutions and social settings" (p. 592). White people are not color blind, unaware of the racist classifications of people, or unconscious of the disproportionate realities between races. An epistemology of ignorance, or a *determined ignorance*, safeguards them.

I'd like to introduce two anecdotes.

A white man gets pissed because I honk at him as he tries to run across the street unexpectedly. "Don't you fucking honk at me you wetback!" As he continues to yell out obscenities and tells me to go "back home," the white man begins to punch my window. My son cries. I am stuck between a trailer in front of me and a vehicle in the back. "What the fuck you going to do boy; do something boy; fucking wetback, do something. Go back to Mexico!" I could see the spectators move into this racist scene. No one is innocent here.

A friend and I take an Uber to a Mexican restaurant. The Uber driver begins to engage in a conversation with us until we arrive at the drive-in. "Yes, can I order some tacos, chalupas, and burritos," I say. The driver turns towards me and says, "Are you Mexican or Hispanic? Because, just a little while ago you were speaking perfect English and then all of a sudden you were like 'chalupa' and 'taco' with a Mexican accent." Whiteness, and all that it encompasses, is that which allows a white individual to feel safe insofar that you speak his or her language. The moment you deviate, his or her principles and pathologies become activated and permit such racializing of bodies to occur.

White Ignorance/Denial, White Arrogance, and White Silence: In "White ignorance," Charles Mills (1997) links white (and moral) ignorance to white supremacy. In historicizing white ignorance, Mill concludes, "White ignorance has been able to flourish all of these years because white epistemology of ignorance has safeguarded . . ." (p. 35). Marilyn Frye (1993) in "On being white" has suggested the term "determined ignorance" (p. 118), while others such as Linda Alcoff address the issue of ignorance by tracing arguments for epistemic ignorance. As Alcoff writes in "Epistemologies of ignorance," the "cognitive norms that produce ignorance as an effect of substantive epistemic practice are those that naturalize and dehistoricize both the process and product of knowing, such that no political reflexivity or sociological analysis is thought to be required or even allowable" (p. 56). Indeed, as Eve Sedgwick (1998) argued in "Privilege of unknowing," ignorance (or the privilege of unknowing) is a powerful epistemological site: "Insofar as ignorance is ignorance of a knowledge—a knowledge that may itself, it goes without saying, be seen as either 'true' or 'false' under some other regime of truth—these ignorances, far from being pieces of the originary dark, are produced by and correspond to particular knowledges and circulate as part of particular regimes of truth" (p. 25). As Elizabeth Spelman writes in "Managing ignorance," ignorance is achieved through a management of not needing to know. The not needing to know leads to white silence. Cris Mayo (2001) in "Civility and its discontents," addresses topics of civility and incivility. In regard to civility, Mayo writes, "As long as one appears sincere in one's ignorance . . . one expects to be forgiven and nurtured into knowledge" (p. 85). Civility is favored because it does not draw attention to the active ignorance. However, incivility is created when "calling into question of why one is pretending not to know" because it reminds the other "that they do already know" (p. 85). Mayo argues incivility is avoided by blaming problems on history rather than on the social actors themselves.

I'd like to conclude here with another anecdote.

A white woman crosses our path as a friend and I exit our vehicle to begin our walk at a park. She eventually asks me what I do. She needed to confirm that by working at the university I meant that I worked in the landscaping department. When addressed, the white woman apologizes and says, "I am sorry, I didn't know." This is not a question of knowing someone's true intentions, but rather, of how their discourse of actions reveals white ignorance and arrogance. The idea of individual ignorance, as Robin DiAngelo (2011) discusses, permits the claims of an un-racialized identity, claims of not belonging to a racial group, and claims of not being part of a "wholly racialized society" (p. 60). The "I didn't know" reinforces the need to know and un-know (Alcoff, 2007, 56; Sedgwick, 1998, p. 25; Tuana, 2006, pp. 3–5; Medina, 2012, p. 32; Frye, 1983, p. 119). As Jose Medina (2012) writes, "the powerful can be spoiled not only by enjoying in a disproportionate way the privilege of knowing (or, rather, being assumed to know), but also by having the privilege of not knowing or of not needing to know" (p. 32). As I corrected the white woman, she enacted a performance of ignorance (I didn't know), which created distance from the very idea that her question could be undergirded by racism. This distancing placed the burden on me to forgive and nurture her into knowledge (Mayo, 2001, p. 85).

White Fragility and White Forgiveness: bell hooks (1989) argues "liberal whites fail to understand how they can and/or do embody white-supremacist values and beliefs even though they may not embrace racism" and "cannot recognize the ways their actions support and affirm the very structure of racist domination and oppression that they profess to wish to see eradicated" (p. 113). White fragility is the claim that one is unable to tolerate racial stress (DiAngelo, 2011, p. 57). White guilt and white forgiveness, as Judy Katz (2003) discusses in *White Awareness*, shoulder the responsibility and burden upon the bodies of color to accept such guilt and issue out forgiveness. This allows the postulation of distance.

In all, what I am arguing is that there is a recipe for making white benevolence that is entangled in imperialist and global designs for maintaining and re-producing power. If white benevolence is reenacted across institutions and social settings, this is because there are principles and pathologies undergirding such actions. The steps that make up this recipe, I argue, suggest an ecology of pathologies and epistemological standpoints that require us to expand the breadth and scope of analysis that we use when we talk about white benevolence. Once we do so, what becomes evident is that even good intentions are entangled and complicit in white supremacy.

WHAT DOES IT MEAN TO LISTEN AND BE MINDFUL OF DIFFERENCE?

Kern: I hear you, Romeo, and so many of the other voices forced to endure such emotional labor. In fact, I think listening is key in writing center work. Especially in terms of difference. And it's never just a matter of listening to words with your ears. To be mindful of difference in terms of equity, accessibility, and equality, we must learn to *listen* with all of our senses. But, I wonder how effective listening can be if there's no action or reaction that stems from that listening. We must be open to actions that positively diminish positions of white benevolence in administrations and beyond. Consider the following scenario.

> *In tutor training, a white/whitely director with so-called good intentions tells the tutors, "You will all have to master and write in Standard Written English (SWE) in order to help others with their writing. We might think of SWE as the paycheck language, because it's how all writ-*

ers succeed in formal settings." A tutor of color turns to their peer and
says, loud enough for the room to hear, "That ain't right." At this stage,
the director confronts the tutor:
>   *Director: What did you say?*
>   *Tutor (addressing the teacher): What'd I say?*
>   *Director: What did you just say?*
>   *Tutor: Oh, I wasn't talking to you.*

In this exchange, the tutor's comment exposes the director's statements as unfounded and unfair, as the director attempts to save face by scolding the tutor. In our scenario, though, the tutor sidesteps further direct action, and potentially weakens the effectiveness of the initial response. In finally claiming, "I wasn't talking to you," the tutor takes a step back toward silence. Don't get me wrong; it's not the tutor's responsibility to take on this emotional labor, and I don't mean to discredit the effectiveness of this performative rhetorical strategy. What I am interested in doing—and I believe it's what this chapter, in part, asks us to consider—is confronting a more direct approach. Why can't the director listen—truly listen—to the given situation with all the faculties and resources available, and then take practical steps to improve? Given the inability to listen and the inevitable inaction, the predictable conclusion is that the director will continue to describe writing in neoliberal/racialized terms and fail to see the damage these so-called good intentions do to both the tutors and writers visiting the center. In a 2015 segment for *MTV News* titled "How Do You Handle a Racist Joke?," Franchesca Ramsey offers the following advice in this order:

1.   The sarcastic approach.
2.   Go completely silent.
3.   Play dumb.
4.   Reply with a judgmental Gif.
5.   Unfriend the offender.
6.   When all else fails, just be honest and direct.

I have no interest in discrediting these first five pieces of advice, either—in fact, to my mind they're all valid rhetorical strategies in terms of anti-racist performance. It's the order with which this advice is presented that concerns me. While acknowledging the very real threat and danger students of color face every day, why must all else fail before direct action becomes a viable option? What happens if we present writers and tutors in our centers with models of mindful listening and direct anti-racist performance? At the very least, we'd offer up space for those performances to be valued as legitimate forms of communication, rather than last resorts.

WHAT DO WE MEAN BY ANTI-RACISM
AND SOCIAL JUSTICE WORK?

Garcia: This is an important conversation and ties back to what you said, Doug, in regard to listening and an ethical praxis of mindfulness of difference. To be mindful of difference is not to engage in excess of difference, or to recognize difference in terms of values of plus- and minus- degree of humanity. Rather, it is to be mindful of other sets of principles of epistemologies that inform literacies and languages. It is to come to terms with and carefully reckon with yourself—to ask, why do I see difference, where do those ideas of difference come from, how is it that I can say I want to hear and see you in and on your own terms and yet the only way for me to hear and see you is for you to enact a bodily performance that is readable to my eyes. The same goes for anti-racism and social justice work, which is not to retrofit or conflate differences, but rather to be open to what all bodies bring to the table. However, to be able to capture this, even if partially, is to be attentive to all bodies and not just some (e.g., a white-Black race paradigm). In addition to the question, I'd like to pose another: "are you actually doing what you say you are doing?" As you might recall, the white writing center director is a cautionary tale of good intentions gone astray. It is not enough to have the intention. These intentions must be carried out with principles of listening and a praxis of mindfulness of difference, and continuously be reflected upon.

Kern: Yes, continuous reflection is key. I don't think enough of us consider the necessary errors or inevitable stumbles that come with anti-racist and social justice work. The point isn't to discourage real efforts toward anti-racist practices and institutions, but, as you note, to reflect upon those moments to help define and subvert setbacks. With this in mind, please forgive just one more scenario, which I share to help illuminate my feelings regarding this question. Let's imagine:

A university writing center invites a renowned scholar to participate in a full day of discussions and talks regarding anti-racism, performance, and language. The day ends with a rhetoric reading group for faculty and other members of the university. Everyone is asked to read and offer feedback on two articles regarding race and gender. At one point during the discussion, the audience is asked to consider what they might have learned from these readings. A white senior faculty member quickly jumps in to respond: "I feel what I've learned from these readings is that I know so very little about Black life. Well, I've seen *The Wire.*"

What can I say? These shallow displays of knowledge surrounding the race and culture of others are innumerable, right? After all, *The Wire*'s white-authored narratives of Black life have been brought into question in both critical and academic circles. So? What's the point, right? What's all of this got to do with anti-racism and social justice? I think we can all agree that the academic's answer in my little narrative was what? Misguided? Still, *The Wire* isn't simply a white-authored narrative of Black life—think of all the Black actors who brought that show to life. To take a case in point, I teach scriptwriting and was fortunate enough to have a co-writer and producer of *The Wire*, George Pelecanos, once join my class as a guest speaker. The first thing he did was show us a dialogue between the characters Avon Barksdale and Stringer Bell. After the clip, he proceeded to tell my students that during the filming of this scene both actors, Idris Elba and Wood Harris, ad-libbed and toyed with the script while shooting it. If we take Pelecanos at his word, does this blur the lines of authorship? And, if so, does it even matter? Here we have a critically acclaimed television show that provided opportunity for a diverse population of actors; and yet, more often than not, the Black characters depicted within *The Wire* are defined by violence and crime. And, as strange as it may sound, here's how my narrative relates to questions surrounding anti-racism and social justice within the academy—People of Color within our institutions are either forced to conform under a false narrative of whitely benevolence, or are defined—by whites—by the violence inflicted upon them by that very same narrative. Consider the other scenarios we've offered up throughout this chapter as we've explored the stories we tell or don't tell in the writing center. When/if "welcomed," People of Color are often exploited, side-stepped, misrepresented, or ignored. Regardless of how you might feel about the white faculty member's statement regarding *The Wire*, the scenario reminds us of why and how simply "talking" about race or difference—without a true commitment to listen and act as a result—simply doesn't cut it.

REFERENCES

Ahmed, S. (2004). *The Cultural Politics of Emotion*. New York: Routledge.

Alcoff, L. Epistemologies of ignorance: Three types. In S. Sullivan & N. Tuana (Eds.), *Race and Epistemologies of Ignorance* (pp. 39–58). New York: SUNY Press.

Andersen, M., Taylor, H., and K. Logio (2016). *Sociology: The Essentials* (9th ed.). Boston: Cengage Learning.

Ansley, F. (1997). White supremacy (and what we should do about it). In R. Delgado & J. Stefancic (Eds.), *Critical White Studies: Looking Behind the Mirror* (pp. 592–593). Philadelphia: Temple University Press.

Arao, B., & Clemens, K. (2013). From safe spaces to brave spaces: A new way to frame dialogue around diversity and social justice. In L.M. Lanreman (Ed.), *The Art of Effective Facilitation: Reflections from Social Justice Eucators* (pp. 135–150). Sterling: Stylus.

Baldwin, J. (2015). *Tell Me How Long the Train's Been Gone*. New York: Library of America.

Barron, N., & Grimm, N. (2002). Addressing racial diversity in a writing center: Stories and lessons from two beginners. *Writing Center Journal, 22*(2), 55–83.

Bawarshi, A., & Pelkowski, S. (1999). Postcolonialism and the idea of a writing center. *Writing Center Journal, 19*(2), 41–58.

Bennet, B. C. (2008). Student rights, home languages, and political wisdom in the writing center. *Writing Lab Newsletter, 32*(5), 7–10.

Bonilla-Silva, E. (2001). *White Supremacy and Racism in the Post-Civil Rights Era*. Boulder: Lynne Rienner Publishers.

Bonilla-Silva, E. (2014). *Racism without Racists: Color-blind Racism and the Persistence of Racial Inequality in America* (4th ed.). Lanham: Rowman & Littlefield.

Brasher, Jordan, Alderman, D., and Inwood, J. (2017). Applying critical race and memory studies to university place naming controversies: Toward responsible landscape policy. *Papers in Applied Geography, 3*(3–4), 292–307.

Carr, L. (1997). *"Colorblind" Racism*. Thousand Oaks: SAGE.

Condon, F. (2007). Beyond the known: Writing centers and the work of anti-racism. *The Writing Center Journal, 27*(2): 19–38.

Cooper, M.M. (1994). Really useful knowledge: A cultural studies agenda for writing centers. *The Writing Center Journal, 14*(2): 97–111.

Davila, B. (2006). Rewriting race in the writing center. *Writing Lab Newsletter, 31*(1), 1–5.

DeCiccio, A. (2012). Can the writing center reverse the new racism? *New England Journal of Higher Education*. Retrieved from http://www.nebhe.org/thejournal/can-the-writing-center-reverse-the-new-racism/

Dees, S., Godbee, B., & Ozias, M. (2007). Navigating conversational turns: Grounding difficult discussions on racism. *Praxis: A Writing Center Journal, 5*(1).

Delgado, R., & Stefancic, J. (2012). *Critical Race Theory: An Introduction* (2nd ed.). New York: New York University Press.

Diab, R., Godbee, B., Ferrel, T., & Simpkins, N. (2012). A multi-dimensional pedagogy for racial justice in writing center. *Praxis: A Writing Center Journal, 10*(1), 1–8.

DiAngelo, R. (2011). White fragility. *International Journal of Critical Pedagogy, 3*(3), 54–70.

Drazler, B. (2007). Social justice in the writing center. *The Peer Review, 1*(2), n.p.

Frankenberg, R. (1993). *White Women, Race Matters: The Social Construction of Whiteness*. Minneapolis: University of Minnesota Press.

Frye, M. (1983). On being white: Thinking toward a feminist understanding of race and race supremacy. In M. Frye (Ed.), *Politics of Reality: Essays in Feminist Theory* (pp. 110–127). Berkeley: The Crossing Press.

Geller, A. E., Condon, F., & Carroll, M. (2011). Bold: The everyday writing center and the production of new knowledge in antiracist theory and practice. In L. Greenfield & K. Rowan (Eds.), *Writing Centers and the New Racism: A Call for Sustainable Dialogue and Change* (pp. 101–123). Logan: Utah State University Press.

Geller, A. E., Eodice, M., Condon, F., Carroll, M., & Boquet, E. H. (2007). *The Everyday Writing Center: A Community of Practice*. Logan: Utah State University Press.

Greenfield, L., & Rowan, K. (Eds.). (2011). *Writing Centers and the New Racism: A Call for Sustainable Dialogue and Change*. Logan: Utah State University Press.

Grimm, N. (1996a). The regulatory role of the writing center: Coming to terms with a loss of innocence. *Writing Center Journal, 17*(1), 5–29.

Grimm, N. (1996b). Rearticulating the work of the writing center. *College Composition and Communication, 47*(4), 523–548.

Grimm, N. (1999). *Good Intentions: Writing Center Work for Postmodern Times*. Portsmouth: Heinemann.

hooks, b. (1989). *Talking Back: Thinking Feminist, Thinking Black*. Cambridge: Ellen Herman and South End Press.

Kail, H., & Trimbur, J. (1987). The politics of peer tutoring. *Writing Program Administration*, *11*(1/2), 5–12.

Katz, J. (2003). *White Awareness: Handbook for Anti-racism Training* (2nd ed.). Norman: University of Oklahoma.

Kendall, F. (2012). *Understanding White Privilege: Creating Pathways to Authentic Relationships Across Race* (2nd ed.). New York: Routledge.

Lunsford, A. (1991). Collaboration, control, and the idea of a writing center. *Writing Center Journal*, *12*(1), 3–10.

Mayo, C. (2001). Civility and its discontents: Sexuality, race, and the lure of beautiful manners. *Philosophy of Education*, 202, 78–87.

McIntosh, P. (1997). White privilege and male privilege: A personal account of coming to see correspondences through work in women's studies. In R. Delgado & J. Stefancic (Eds.), *Critical White Studies: Looking Behind the Mirror* (291–299). Philadelphia: Temple University Press.

Medina, J. (2012). *The Epistemology of Resistance: Gender and Racial Oppression, Epistemic Injustice, and Resistant Imaginations*. Oxford: Oxford University Press.

Mills, C. (1997). *The Racial Contract*. Ithaca: Cornell University Press.

Museus, S.D. (2015). Racism and racial equity in higher education. *Ashe Higher Education Report*, *42*(1), 1–112.

Ozias, M., & Godbee, B. (2011). Organizing for antiracism in writing centers: Principles for enacting social change. In L. Greenfield & K. Rowan (Eds.), *Writing Centers and the New Racism: A Call for Sustainable Dialogue and Change* (pp. 150–176). Logan: Utah State University Press.

Pulido, L. (2009). Rethinking environmental racism: White privilege and urban development in Southern California. In J. Radway, K. Gaines, B. Shank, & P. Eschen (Eds.), *American Studies: An Anthology* (pp. 465–475). West Sussex: Wiley-Blackwell.

Ramsey, F. (2015). How Do You Handle a Racist Joke? *YouTube*, uploaded by *MTV News*, 1 July 2015, https://www.youtube.com/watch?v=Bg1aTLsS69Y&t=152s.

Sedgwick, E. (1998). Privilege of unknowing. *Genders*, *1*, 102–124.

Spelman, E. (2007). Managing ignorance. In S. Sullivan & N. Tuana (Eds.), *Race and Epistemologies of Ignorance* (pp. 119–131). New York: SUNY Press.

Sue, D. (2003). *Overcoming Our Racism: The Journey to Liberation*. San Francisco: Jossey-Bass.

Sullivan, S., & and Tuana, N. (Eds.). (2007). *Race and Epistemologies of Ignorance*. Albany: State University of New York Press.

Till, K. (2012). Wounded cities: Memory-work and a place-based ethics of care. *Political Geography*, *31*(3), 3–14.

Tuana, N. (2006). The speculum of ignorance: The women's health movement and epistemologies of ignorance. *Hypatia*, *21*(3), 1–19.

Villanueva, V. (2006). Blind: Talking about the new racism. *Writing Center Journal*, *26*(1), 3–19.

Weaver, M. (2006). A call for racial diversity in the writing center. In C. Murphy & B. Stay (Eds.), *The Writing Center Director's Resource Book* (pp. 79–92). Mahwah: Lawrence Erlbaum Associates.

Wellman, D. (1993). *Portraits of White Racism* (2nd ed.). Cambridge: Cambridge University Press.

Zhang, P., St. Amand, J., Quaynor, J., Haltiwanger, T., Chambers, E., Canino, G., & Ozias, M. (2013). "Going there": Peer writing consultants' perspectives on the new racism and peer writing pedagogies. *Across the Disciplines: A Journal of Language, Learning, and Academic Writing*, *10*(3). Retrieved from http://wac.colostate.edu/atd/race/oziasetal/family.cfm.

6

WHITE BENEVOLENCE
Why Supa-save-a-Savage Rhetoric Ain't Getting It

Wonderful Faison, Romeo García, and Anna K. Treviño

Dear Reader,

Romeo, Wonderful, and I have written together in support of each other. We have different voices and different but related things to say. We believe saying them together matters. We also hope that you learn from our work, but if there is one thing we want to emphasize, it is that there is no one solution nor one single voice that can work to fight against white supremacy. Just as there is no one solution, we don't reach just one conclusion. We believe this is valid and understand that we are disregarding certain conventions. Ultimately, we believe that this unconventional approach offers more to you than it asks of you. If you consider yourself a conventional reader, we challenge you to stretch and step, even just a little, beyond the boundaries of the epistemologies on which you rely.

LET'S BEGIN: AMERICA, THE LAND OF THE FREE AND THE HOME OF THE BRAVE, RIGHT?

While there are many epistemologies, not all are valued equally nor wield the same amount of power. In the U.S., the dominant epistemology (of white privilege) reflects and reproduces "covert and overt assumptions regarding White superiority, territorial expansion, and 'American' democratic ideals such as meritocracy, objectivity, and individuality" (Delgado Bernal, 2002, p. 111). Such ideals and assumptions provide white people with the privilege to insist that race is not/ no longer an issue in the U.S., as well as the privilege to insist that the dominant epistemology is not only the norm, but also the only epistemology—invalidating and ignoring the experiences of People of Color. However, systems of knowing (epistemologies) are not only raced, they are intersectional—also gendered, classed, abled, sexual, and so on—because they are "linked to worldviews based on the conditions under which people live and learn" (Delgado Bernal, 2002, p. 106).

https://doi.org/10.7330/9781646421534.c006

The role race plays in shaping white women's epistemologies is crucial to this chapter primarily because as U.S. history and our present day show, when presented with the choice, white women align along racial lines over gendered lines. The role race plays in shaping white women's epistemologies is also crucial because the dominant epistemology supports, validates, and encourages White Womanhood Benevolence based on the assumption that whites are superior to all other races and ethnicities; therefore, all non-white/racialized people need help achieving to and succeeding in their level of excellence—*to be saved.*

In the following sections, we will explore how white women often view the language and linguistic practices of the Colored body, as well as the Colored body and its related epistemologies, not as that which can challenge and reconceive the way the academy conceives of and produces academic writing, but as that which can still be studied and researched as a non-normative discourse practice, needing to be "refined" and "polished." In the first section, Willow highlights the ways in which an epistemology of white benevolence functions as a gatekeeping tactic as those embodying it (mostly, but not always white women) either misconstrue or fail to understand why WOC purposefully reject and resist such epistemology in the work they do. White benevolence cannot read these acts of rejection and resistance on the terms set out by WOC, and instead read them as acts that purport less rigorous *standards* and conventions, or merely leads the benevolent to conclude that WOC *just don't get it* or *just don't know how to communicate effectively.*

WHOSE EPISTEMOLOGY IS IT ANYWAY?

"What do students need in order to succeed in college (and beyond)?"

Most people asking the question above, for whatever reason, genuinely want to help students succeed. I know I sure as hell do. But I also know, from the scholarship, from conversations, from my own experiences as a Chicana student, teacher, and teacher/student/writing consultant in writing classes that this seemingly innocent desire to help, the way this desire to help and the reason this desire to help is seen as a noble cause can be problematic as fuck. Because helping others is known to be a good thing, we often don't look critically to consider from where the driving force and the mechanisms behind the concept of helpfulness in academia comes.

So, while many people attempt to answer this question with replicable, generalizable solutions using the words attrition, retention, persistence, and completion (at times, myself included), we forget that we are embodying certain epistemologies. For example, if a professor or researcher is attempting to figure out what minoritized students need to succeed, but is informed by the dominant U.S. epistemology previously discussed. This deficit perspective is well-documented in rhetoric and writing studies and writing centers. Uncoincidentally, we are in a field that is composed predominantly of white women. It should come as no surprise that I have witnessed white benevolence in action in classrooms and writing centers and have been taught to perpetuate it.

The typical writing center and classroom positions whiteness as The Standard; however, this standard is unjust and has led to "the histories, experiences, cultures, and languages of students of color [to be] devalued, misinterpreted, or omitted within formal educational settings" (Delgado Bernal, 2002, p. 105). Thus, white women working from a place of white benevolence believe that students of color just need help becoming white: learning and adhering to the white rhetorical tradition, as well as enacting acceptable white ways of writing and researching. Unfortunately for the students who desire to learn more than white ways, to do more than reproduce systems that work to delegitimize them, the professors and administrators functioning from this epistemology invest their time and energy into visions of student success that deny student agency and epistemological justice.

White ignorance masked under the guise of benevolence encodes everything of and about me in order protect whiteness. My closeness to my research interests is read as a lack of objectivity—*mesearch*. Thus, any claims I make about whiteness or injustices can be easily dismissed. The ground for this dismissal, of course, is not typically seen for what it is, but rather a learning moment for me; it's not about my work, *per se*, but how I go about it or how I sound when I present it, and I just need to be taught how to do that better. It's almost like white conventions are really about white feelings and comfort. As a Chicana in academia, I am supposed to let the good white people help me, making them feel good about themselves.

When I refuse to play along, my resistance and unwillingness are read as a lack of intelligence and/or ability, motivation, or even so as ungracious. Never fear, white benevolence will always also be *kind enough* to inform me that I am here because they let me be here: setting expectations and boundaries is not my job. It is my job to rise up to The Standard, and white benevolence is supposed to be what gets me there.

I'M NOT YOUR AUNT JEMIMA: DOUBLE-CONSCIOUSNESS, WHITE BENEVOLENCE, AND WHITE WOMANHOOD

These epistemologies that white women use—the epistemologies of white womanhood/motherhood—are enacted onto the Black body, often under the guise of white benevolence. This notion of benevolence, charitable giving, or philanthropy began in antebellum America. The act of benevolence and charity is often critiqued by those who are tasked with being the most charitable (the rich). For the most benevolent, charity functioned most often as an anatomy of suspicion, promoting elaborate rituals of authentication (Rayn, 2000, p. 686).

When I was in a Predominantly White Writing Center, and I worked in many, I often found myself feeling like a unicorn. It benefited the Predominantly White Writing Center to have me, but the cost of being the one relegated not only to critiquing, researching, and publishing on the racial, if not racist implications of the Predominantly White Writing Center, was at a great intellectual and emotional cost—a cost I had to pay. However, at times, that same Predominantly White Writing Center with those same predominantly white tutors and directors, often put little work into either relieving my emotional labor or helping to equally disperse the intellectual labor.

Yet, many of these so called "allies" benefited from my labor because it allowed them to suggest they were actively engaging in anti-racist writing center research and praxis—research and praxis in which they cared not to engage any more than pointing to the one Black person in their center engaging in such work. And yet, I had to exult the writing center as some happy home without very real social problems. I had to masquerade—to be someone's Aunt Jemima. This facade often left me feeling anger, resentment, and outright contempt, not only for the writing center, but also the safe and welcoming space it purported to be. I wondered about these promoted and elaborate rituals of authentication and regulation, where "commentators both relied on and mistrusted the body as a legible index of need, returning to it endlessly in their descriptions of worthy and unworthy supplicants, but also warning of its many deceptions. Disability, after all, could be faked, as could illness, hunger pains, and other sympathy-eliciting elements" (Rayn, 2000, p. 686).

When such concerns are placed on the colored or Black body as Melville does in *The Confidence-Man: His Masquerade*, "the epistemology of doing good" becomes intertwined "with the question of 'knowing' blackness" (Rayn, 2000, p. 686). Part of "knowing blackness" for white womanhood, I argue, is believing that People of Color (POC), and specifically Black people, lack certain literacy skills and need their assistance in accessing those skills. However, the Black body also becomes a site of interrogation to ensure it meets certain white standards of appropriateness.

This appropriateness asks that Black women take care of the emotional and intellectual needs of the white woman—to educate her on the operations of Black women—so that she, that white woman, can speak "objectively" about her Black friend, mentor, colleague, etc. Furthermore, this appropriateness asks that we temper our temper at systemic oppressions disregarding many of our own realities that "*to be a Negro in this country and to be relatively conscious, is to be in a rage almost all the time*" (Baldwin, 1961, p. 205).

YOU FORGOT MAMMY HAD A BRAIN: DISSECTING WHITE WOMANHOOD

As a woman, white womanhood demands I support the feminist fight for economic equality and individualism alongside white men, while she turns a blind eye to the oppressive systems that rip the Black family apart. White womanhood asks that we love, trust, uphold, and take care of the white patriarchy and its standards, while simultaneously using our sons, fathers, and husbands as scapegoats for the barbary of the white patriarchy. I watch as white women justify the slaughter of unarmed Black men by white cops; I watch as white women tutors get upset at Black clients for not "seeing how much they are trying to help them." I watch as white tutors fail to address racist comments white male clients make about POCs in their writing; they clutch their pearls in horror but refuse to show clients how their writing is an act of violence and terrorism.

White womanhood asks not that I, as a lesbian, conform to more stringent forms of heterosexuality, but that I remain silent, and become an invisible, desexualized/asexualized listener to its wants and desires. White heterosexual women demand this silence because sex is always already white and I must watch myself, lest my vocalization of sexual desire become susceptible to the white imaginary describing Black sex as barbaric, rough, animalistic. White women and whiteness in the writing center hold and police the status of objective judgement, specifically over and against Black bodies.

As a Black consultant, white womanhood asks that I conform to ideas of motherliness that are rooted in guiding and often either infantilizing or fetishizing the literacy skills of historically marginalized populations. It asks that I be less vocal about some of the mistakes teachers make, i.e., writing unclear assignments, providing feedback that uses hollow words of critique like "vague," etc. It claims I must help clients "argue" through written discourse in measured tones, without encouraging and showing historically marginalized clients how to use the different forms of argumentation from their various cultures in their writing. Essentially, white womanhood asks that Black women acquiesce to the white ideologies around marginalized populations to gain both acceptance and support.

It is this need for both acceptance (for their objectivity on Black bodies) and acquiescence that creates a double consciousness in me as a Black lesbian writing center (WC) consultant. This double consciousness creates a struggle to (1) refrain from being the white woman's Aunt Jemima by accepting her critiques of the written discourse(s) of Black people as non-standard, alternative, etc., (2) to decide, based on my own standards of appropriateness, what the white woman should know about the Black woman and how she forms discourse, and (3) to push against the use of marginalized linguistic writing skills as markers of deficiency to be used as examples of writing styles consultants must change/fix, and (4) to disrupt and undo homogenized notions of appropriate forms of academic discourse.

At best, white womanhood asks that I play Native informer, and inform not only historically marginalized clients about the ways of white (academic) writing, but also to inform the white matriarchy of their submission/compliance to these ways of writing. At worst, it asks that I comply, stay quiet, and do not rock the academic-writing boat, lest white women lose their identities as writing consultants par excellence.

I AM NOT YOUR NATIVE INFORMANT!

Will there ever have been a time, in the past or present, to think of the writing center (WC) as anything but a wound(ed/ing) place (see Till, 2012; Brasher et al., 2017)? Some will continue to argue that the WC is in a unique position, for it occupies an in-between space, it is a border(ed)land essentially, demarcated on one end by capital [I]nstitution and the capital [C]lassroom. And yet, there will never be a time that it is not entangled and/or complicit in the microcosmic reproduction of society: power structures, power differentials, human capital. There will never be a time that capital [WC] cannot be thought of as a prism through which to see the opening, closing, and policing of the WC *border(ed)land* and *community*; a community that functions as a knowledge apparatus that is subsumed into power structures, power differentials, and human capital; a community that was founded on the principle of the expropriation of land and policing of land, resources, and people. The WC continues to confront an impasse, however, that drives white benevolence: how to overcome the pervasiveness of whiteness that keeps the (colonial) wound open? There will never be a time, though, where whiteness can be thought of as something detached from white bodies; a careful reckoning will always be needed. And yet, what we have witnessed is that anti-racism and social justice put on something like a new shirt. Will there ever have been a time, in the past or present, to deny this move as anything but a cloaking of an epistemological crisis facing white bodies? No!

The aporia of WCs is an irresistible power of desire. The desire, for instance, to adopt frameworks, concepts, and projects to present the illusion that the WC can rewrite itself beyond colonial. The WC has needed such illusions to sustain itself. Yet, the reality within that illusion is that the WC desires to know cultural difference and to foreclose upon that difference. From WC mottos and philosophies to WC practices and theories, there is the desire to manage and control the flow and circulation of bodies and ideas. This is an ethos and ethics inherited from a constellation of stories and genealogies that has as its topos intelligibility, rationale, and totality. This is the telos of Western epistemology. Ironically, thus, in sort of a transcendental pursuit of deconstructing the WC as "centre," the WC rewrites itself as colonial, for its very design as "center" is fraught. The WC cannot solve its colonial problem, a problem created by the very act of interpolation cloaked by an articulative rhetoric of salvation, progress, and development (e.g., modernity). It cannot solve it because it has as its foundation benevolence as its historical problem and possible resolution. If we can disinvent this kind of narrative, we can be more forthright that any condition of possibility in the WC is also its condition of impossibility. I hope to illuminate this in two scenarios: (1) consultant-to-consultant and (2) face-to-face consultations.

Will there ever have been a time, in the past or present, when a *native informant* actually existed? Some experiences cannot be understood and archived. Many, however, are quick to turn to Krista Ratcliffe's term, rhetorical listening, which she describes as: (a) a "trope for interpretive invention . . . a code for cross-cultural conduct" (1), (b) a "stance of openness that a person may choose to assume in relation to any person, text, or culture" (17), and (c) an ethic of care and a responsible commitment (34) that "[t]urns hearing (a reception process) into invention (a production process)" (46). The impasse the WC faces is similar to the one those adopting Ratcliffe's term must carefully reckon with: an epistemological crisis ("a stance of openness"). What we find is a term, much like a body, haunted by a whiten(ed/ing) disposition (to read the *othered* body), benevolence (to be open to the *othered* body), and gazing (to see and hear the *othered* body in and on their own terms): a listening that takes place in a space (an imagining space) that is first and foremost, in service to oneself; a service that confirms the *other's* own alterity, their own difference. Might it ever be possible to learn how to be in service, otherwise? Not when there is a foreclosing on the *other*.

Yet, within the WC, there is a continuous literature dedicated to knowing the *other*. However we cut it, be it projects of anti-racism and social justice or methodological approaches grounded in critical race theory or emic/etic perspectives, there is a desire in WCs to know cultural difference and to foreclose upon that difference. And herein lies the predicament of white epistemologies, approaching the *other* as native informer.

> *Scene 1*: A conversation unfolds between two consultants, one white and one a person of color, and the white consultant asks, "please forgive me for my ignorance, but help me understand better your experiences and your community."
>
> *Scene 2*: A consultant of color is working with a white student in a face-to-face conversation, and the topic of conversation is on racial issues in a Trump era. The white student states, "I've never been a racist," and asks, "how can I prove to people that I am not a racist because it is not my fault I am white?"

In both scenes, we could say there is a display of good intentions. In scene 1 the white consultant expresses both a kind of guilt for their white ignorance and an interest in understanding the consultant of color's experiences. In scene 2, the white student is asking for help in demonstrating to others that they are not racist. In both scenes, the consultant of color is called upon as a native informer, to disclose information and to guide the white benevolent social actor. While this may seem inconsequential, there is something to be said about the exchange between the benevolent transparent intellectual and the native informant.[1]

One question that comes to mind is, would scene 1 or scene 2 play out if the consultant of color had been white? Another question to ask includes, is the white consultant prepared not only to listen and respond, but also act upon a call to action? I pose both questions not to undermine the very real anti-racist and social justice work white folks are doing in the WC. Rather, what I am trying to illuminate in the two WC scenes is the intricate relationship between desire, interest, and

---

1. See Gayatri Spivak (1999) for more insight on how the "native informant" is a "mark of expulsion" and a mark of "crossing out the impossibility of the ethical relation" (pp. 5–6).

power that plays out in white benevolence. I am reminded of Gayatri Spivak and her central question of whether the subaltern can speak and be heard? Spivak (1994) acknowledges that the subaltern indeed "produces a constant interruption for the full telos of Reason and capitalism" (p. 55). Her concern, though, is with how the subaltern is interpolated through "totalizing concepts of power and desire" (1988, p. 74) and how the "subaltern's inability to speak is predicated upon an attempt to speak" in which "no appropriate response can be proffered" (1994, p. 62). The very act of calling upon the "native informer" and providing them a space from which to speak assumes that the impossibility of communication can be overcome. That is to say, Spivak is not contesting the literal question, "can the subaltern speak and be heard?" Rather, she is challenging the desire, interest, and power dynamics that compel the act to know cultural difference and to foreclose upon that difference.

Scene 1 and scene 2 provide a contextual reference to understand the interconnection between desire, interests, and power as it informs the subject-object relationship. That is to say, whether in the context of WC policy or face-to-face consultations, both are overdetermined by a history that is colonial and hierarchical. The very utterances of "please forgive me for my ignorance" (scene 1) or "I've never been a racist" ignores, however, the historical tropes of whiteness. Once more, I turn to Spivak to help explain the detriment of white benevolence. In "Responsibility," she identifies two entities, the World Bank and the Green Party, that for all purposes claim they act in the name of the people. Spivak (1994) offers the following words:

> In order to hear him [native informant], 'Europe' would need him to represent responsibility, by reflex, in 'Europe's' way. In other words, he would have to change his mind-set. That is how the old colonial subject was shaped. When we do it, we call it education.

While scenes 1 and 2 only offer minimal information, they call upon the native informant to engage in a felicitous performance that pleases the desire and interests of the white benevolent subject. Thus, even if the intentions are good, as evident in both scenes, the subaltern is rendered silent, for their structures of thought and feeling are but a mere interpolation in the ways of management and control of the flow and circulation of bodies and ideas. And because the mere utterance of words demonstrates for the white benevolent subject an act of speech and listening, they claim this to be a victory along the lines of responsible anti-racism and social justice work without regard to how the heterogenous native informant is reduced both in identity and space of difference. In doing so, an inheritance of Western epistemology reproduces the subject-object correlation.

In scenes 1 and 2, there is a Western praxis in play. It is difficult to not acknowledge the subject-object relationship and racial grammar being reinvented within such contexts. For so long the white benevolent subject has had the privilege of knowing and not needing to know (see Medina, 2012) and of placing the burden on the person of color to nurture them into knowledge (see Mayo, 2001). Such white ignorance, symptomatic of a pathology of whiteness, normalizes these behaviors as non-colonial and non-racist (DiAngelo, 2011). However, when Charles Mills (1997) argues that not all white people are signatories, but rather beneficiaries of a system of institutions of white belonging and white entitlements (p. 11), he was articulating how benevolence supports and affirms "the very structure of racist domination and oppression" that white benevolent subjects "profess to wish to see eradicated" (hooks, 1989, p. 113). This is because, as Bonilla-Silva (2012) would argue, there exists a racial grammar, one that displays white arrogance and white fragility as the summation of white benevolent epistemology. As I redirect you, the reader, to scene 1 and scene 2, I want you to consider how forecasting of ignorance and claims of non-racism illuminate the overdetermined history of the WC that is colonial and hierarchical. As Ahmed (2004) argues, these declarative modes involve a "fantasy of transcendence in which 'what' is transcended is the very 'thing' admitted to in the declaration" (n.p.). If the WC will always rewrite itself as colonial, where does that leave us, then, with regard to a hope for a different WC?

If the question at this moment remains, "should WCs be involved in research that brings whiteness to the forefront?" then the point is missed. What I am calling attention to is the kind of desire and interests that only contribute to rewriting the WC as colonial—recentering colonial logics of management and control. On an evolutionary continuum, we have the following in the WC: white benevolence; white benevolent subjects saving themselves; white benevolent subjects savings the "other"; white benevolent subjects educating others on how to do anti-racist and social justice work. So what hope is there, especially in the context of anti-racism, anti-colonialist, and anti-imperialist discourse? Considering what Spivak (1994) says about responsibility, that "There can be no assumption that 'pure' responsibility can appear, unstructured and unstaged" (p. 45), and, that "All responsibility is a simulacrum of responsibility" (p. 59), I believe we need to develop in the WC what Spivak (1988) calls a theory of ideology. If we continue to ignore the interconnection between desire, interests, and power as it informs the subject-object relationship, we risk a "dangerous utopianism" (p. 85). And within such a theory of ideology, we must strive to detach the rhetoric of salvation, progress, and development from denominations of responsibility. At every turn made within anti-racist and social justice work, there must be a persistent position of critique.

I am proposing a relational framework of ethics and responsibility that works to disinvent the discourse of Western epistemology. I, a person of color, cannot be your native informant of history or your source of information, for even as I speak, I am only identifiable through those chains of definitive descriptions and significations that are produced in discursive discourses of self and the other (Spivak, 1999, p. 49). A relational framework of ethics and responsibility breaks from purely academic praxis and shifts towards Indigenous discussions of relational forms of knowing and connectedness (see Wilson, 2009; Chilisa, 2012; Smith, 2012). It approaches the opportunity to get to "work" as relationship-building. But it does not ignore the role of desire, interest, and power, nor the very reality that the WC will write and rewrite itself as colonial. One might ask, thus, is it possible for the WC to be anything but colonial. Unless we are willing to forego the very *idea of the WC*, the answer remains. The challenge is going forth cognizant that "all responsibility is a simulacrum of responsibility," but also recognizing that all "complicities within this necessity are not equivalent" (Spivak, 1994, p. 59). Much work is left to be done, but that work begins with relationship-building in and on everyone's own terms and not just white benevolent subjects.

The WC is a wound(ed/ing) place that will never be able to rid itself of its (colonial) memories, of the traces of those who have arrived (physically), not yet arrived (physically), and those who will never have arrived. *The idea of the WC,* which came into existence under the university, is entangled and/or complicit in the microcosmic reproduction of society (power structures, power differentials, human capital). *The idea of the WC* connotes specific things: (1) a dwelling place that is not mine, (2) a space built on the notion of absences and insufficiency, (3) a space where I must ask permission to enter, to be seen, to be heard, and (4) a space that attempts to overcome its histories and erase its memory, all the while foreclosing on the *other.* So, take for instance the very utterance "can you help me?" This moment cannot be read as some simple projection of academic insecurity; we have to see that moment as the arrivant confronting their own alterity, as you, the WC tutor, reaffirm, vis-à-vis the only response that can be proffered (yes I can help you), their *otherness*—how might we respond differently?

Some years ago, I wrote "Un-making Gringo-Centers" for those who have arrived (policed in Gringodemia), those who have not arrived (screened at the border), those who will never have arrived (imprisoned by an imaginary, monsterized by encounters and interactions, and shackled by internal and external oppressions). The WC, I argued, is not a safe space, and hence, it cannot and should not be protected. Will there ever have been a time, in the past or present, in which I can say, I have arrived? I have hope. But not the kind of hope so often expressed within *the idea of higher education*. Returning home, vis-à-vis *community listening* (see García, 2018), it is a hope for that which may or may not arrive: "a hope that one might live another day, that one makes a choice to live another day, with another option, in the face of a forced choice, which is not a choice at all but a demand" (García & Cortez, 2020).

CONCLUDING REMARKS: WE SAID WHAT WE SAID

Romeo: I cannot be your native informant of history, your source of information, for even as I speak, I am only identifiable through those chains of definitive descriptions (Spivak, 1999, p. 49) and significations that are produced in discursive discourses of self and the other. Moreover, my sense of ethical and social responsibility is to not purchase or deploy that rhetoric or narrative of reductionism of a people with whom I share a genealogy. Rather, my disposition is to hold people accountable and to work toward a relational framework of ethics and responsibility. At once, such a framework recognizes the inescapability of our complicities and our capacities to know and not know. It also acknowledges the need for relationship-building. But all of this must be undergirded not by a sense of urgency, but rather, a sense of ethics and responsibility that begs the question, "for what reason and toward what ends?"

Wonderful: What we ask for is a shift from white benevolence to *collaborative benevolence*. Humans are social beings; we grow and sustain one another through acts of togetherness, resistance, and assistance. Essentially, everyone needs assistance to achieve both societal and self-growth. For those who have gained access to what they want and what they desire through these societal acts, helping reshape norms, standards, and even acts of resistance, they must and should give back to the society from which we all benefit. They must and should assist others in reaching their potential, no matter how limited or limitless it may be.

Writing is a social act, one that is culturally situated and produced. One that changes with the needs of society. One that is regulated, most often, by those who benefit the most from the needs of society. However, the potential to expand academic discourse is as limitless as the potential of the clients we serve. In writing, the goal of collaborative benevolence is to work with clients, to engage and form bonds with them through listening to their stories, being explicit about the ways academic writing can silence their stories if they do not learn certain rhetorical moves, and showing clients the choices they can make in writing, i.e., adding their own linguistic writing moves to help support their claims. Writing is also a social act that requires acts of togetherness.

Willow: As Romeo and Wonderful have pointed out, relationship-building and collaboration are essential because writing is a social act. Writing centers and classrooms are spaces of possibilities for both; however, it is also important to keep in mind that epistemological justice is required for such acts and work. White benevolence and epistemological justice cannot coexist.

All: For our proposed means and ends, white benevolence must end because it simply will no longer do.

Sincerely,
Not the Breakfast Club (White Kids)

REFERENCES

Ahmed, S. (2004). Declarations of whiteness: The non-performativity of anti-racism. *Borderlands, 3*(2), 1–15.

Bernal, D. D. (2002). Critical race theory, latino critical theory, and critical raced-gendered epistemologies: Recognizing students of color as holders and creators of knowledge. *Qualitative Inquiry, 8*(1), 105–126. https://doi.org/10.1177/107780040200800107.

Bonilla-Silva, E. (2012). The invisible weight of whiteness: The racial grammar of everyday life in contemporary America. *Ethnic and Racial Studies, 35*(2), 173–194. https://doi.org/10.1080/01419870.2011.613997.

Brasher, J., Alderman, D., and Inwood, J. (2017). Applying critical race and memory studies to university place naming controversies: Toward responsible landscape policy. *Papers in Applied Geography, 3*(3–4), 292–307.

Chilisa, B. (2012). *Indigenous Research Methodologies.* Los Angeles, CA: Sage.

DiAngelo, R. (2011). White fragility. *International Journal of Critical Pedagogy, 3*(3), 54–70.

García, R. (2018). "Creating presence from absence and sound from silence." *Community Literacy Journal, 13*(1), 2018, pp. 7–15.

García, R., & Cortez, J. (Forthcoming). The trace of a mark that scatters. *Rhetoric Society Quarterly.*

hooks, b. (1989). *Talking Back: Thinking Feminist, Thinking Black.* Cambridge: Ellen Herman and South End Press.

Mayo, C. (2001). Civility and its discontents: Sexuality, race, and the lure of beautiful manners. In S. Rice (Ed.), *Philosophy of Education Yearbook 2001* (pp. 78–87). Champaign, IL: University of Illinois at Urbana-Champaign.

Medina, J. (2012). *The Epistemology of Resistance: Gender and Racial Oppression, Epistemic Injustice, and Resistant Imaginations.* Oxford: Oxford University Press.

Mills, C. (1997). *The Racial Contract.* Ithaca, NY: Cornell University Press.

Ratcliffe, C. (2005). *Rhetorical Listening: Identification, Gender, and Whiteness.* Southern Illinois University Press.

Smith, L. T. (2013). *Decolonizing Methodologies: Research and Indigenous Peoples* (2nd Edition). Zed Books.

Spivak, G. (1988). Can the Subaltern Speak? In C. Nelson & L. Grossberg (Eds.), *Marxism and the Interpretation of Culture* (pp. 271–313). Urbana, IL: University of Illinois Press.

Spivak, G. (1994). "Responsibility." *Boundary 2, 21*(3), 19–64. https://doi.org/doi:10.23 07/303600

Spivak, G. (1999). *A Critique of Postcolonial Reason: Toward a History of the Vanishing Present.* Harvard University Press.

Till, K. (2012). Wounded cities: Memory-work and a place-based ethics of care. *Political Geography, 31*(3), 3–14.

Wilson, S. (2008). *Research Is Ceremony: Indigenous Research Methods.* Fernwood Publishing.

7

SPIRITUAL BYPASSING IN THE WRITING CENTER

Mitzi Ceballos, Wonderful Faison, and Bernice Olivas

What is the damage to allyship when the "ally" is embodied in a white female body—the same body that systemically and purposefully continues to uphold white supremacy through silence, disregard, and willful ignorance? What price is paid by the Black, Brown, and Indigenous people who bear the burden of remaining pleasant in the face of racism, misogynoir, and crippling bigotry just to get by? What, indeed, is done to the psyche of the racial minority?

MITZI

I worked at my undergraduate writing center for four years, with predominantly white coworkers who did research on social justice–oriented topics and who believed grammar to be a colonial construct that they said they refused to reinforce. But they were also coworkers who gave me nicknames like "Angry Latina," and, so I'm told, would call me "that crazy bitch obsessed with being oppressed." They were the ones who rolled their eyes when I spoke too much in our meetings, and they exchanged looks when I entered the room.

All of this might have been a little more bearable if I had had a white ally in the director. But the director, needless to say, seemed to lack the time needed for running a writing center *and* addressing the white supremacy and privilege the center was built upon. The director had a soft voice, a fun personality, a non-threatening appearance. Her office door was always open, and she was always willing to hear me out on any current predicament. We spoke often. Looking back, I think she might have interpreted her willingness to talk as leaning into the discomfort of anti-racist work.

Our conversations almost always followed a pattern: either she would block off time in my tutoring schedule without consulting me first, or

https://doi.org/10.7330/9781646421534.c007

I'd unapologetically enter her office. She would shut the door. I would proceed to carefully and professionally deliver my information, taking care not to show negative emotion or to use the offending coworker's name. The director might ask a clarifying question or two. And then, the magic trick.

The director would pull some rhetorical maneuver or other to distract me from my anger and pain. We'd talk about the invisibility of privilege: "It's certainly not their fault that they don't know these things, right? They didn't mean to hurt you." Or "The thing about writing centers is that we have a whole new cohort of tutors every year, so it's impossible to have everyone on the same page when it comes to these things." Finally, if I was lucky that day, she would offer a solution. For example, she decided to implement an assignment wherein tutors-in-training would have the option of reading pieces authored by my own heroes, Victor Villanueva and Romeo Garcia. I would then leave her office feeling heavy and guilty for being such a problem child. I would make excuses. How can I expect to be understood, I remember asking myself, if there is only one of me to understand? For three years, I was the only Latine in that center. *I* barely understood my place in the university, academy, writing center. I thought it was my duty to explain myself, and I was doing it poorly.

The next stage came at night, maybe the next morning. It would hit me: the solution wasn't a solution at all, it wasn't even a beginning. The director had hurt the only Latina, and when deciding whether or not the white tutors needed to learn a few things to stop hurting the Latina, she decided to give them the option. She would protect them, and herself, from the discomfort of grappling with their white privilege, but would not protect me from the racism that was slowly crushing me.

A few times, I thought about quitting. But always, I remembered the writers. The young Latines who shared their writing with me, spoke Spanish with me, trusted me. One student said they had been considering dropping out but stayed because our tutoring sessions made them feel like they belonged. Another Latina liked talking to me about what it felt like to be the only person of color in the room. So I stayed.

In the fourth year of my writing center experience, I changed. I was a second-year McNair Scholar, which meant I was finishing research and applying to graduate programs. The added workload and stress overfilled my cup, and my body began to respond differently to the writing center. It was no longer cold and unflinching; I started getting at least one nosebleed inside the center each week, and on days when too many white coworkers let a microaggression slip I had to step out to battle either tears or nausea. But something else was different. I knew I was leaving soon. Knowing I had my foot out the door, I embraced my temporary state. I had power.

I utilized that power during the last few conversations with the director. On one final occasion, I noticed that she had blocked off a half-hour from my schedule. I prepared myself; I held my head high and entered her office in a controlled but underlying rage, ready for her manipulations and rhetorical games. When I entered her office, with its soft blanket on her chair, the awards and stuffed unicorn plushies, she did not shut the door. That was the first shock. And then, she acknowledged that I had endured racism and struggles. And she apologized.

Before I could process what had just occurred, she said but, *but* I would have to endure racism everywhere I went, even in my graduate program. The woman who, upon learning that one of her employees had called me the Angry Latina, who had told me that she would not intervene on personal matters, was now saying that she wanted to ensure I had the tools I needed to handle the oppression as I entered my new identity as a graduate student. She asked me if there was anything I wanted to tell her. I got up and shut her office door myself. There was much to tell, but I settled on telling her that I had noticed whenever I discussed anything having to do with privilege, even if it had nothing to do with her, even if I wasn't speaking to her, her body language clearly stated she was uncomfortable. I could be explaining the term "white feminism" to someone, and if she heard me, she would avoid making eye contact with me, twisted her hands, displayed a panicked facial expression. *This is who you are,* I was saying. She did not deny my accusation.

"I am allowed to be uncomfortable," she said, her tone defensive. It was the closest thing to anger that I'd ever heard in her.

"Yes, but you prioritize your comfort over my humanity."

I have not forgotten the look on her face when I said that. To tell the truth, I have not forgotten anything, as much as I would have liked to. I said I had power; it turns out power is a fleeting thing. The first few months of my life as a graduate student belonged to the writing center director, tucked away in one of her boxes besides the stuffed unicorns. I gave her one of those unicorns, back in the beginning when I briefly thought I belonged in that center. Miles away from her, I still performed autopsies on our words, over and over: I came up with responses and I used the things I've learned in my graduate seminars to explain the director's behavior. I saw a therapist. She told me that when I found myself returning to that office with the closed door, to write my thoughts down and keep moving. I have put physical distance between us, my therapist said. Now for the spiritual.

What happens when we are left feeling unheard? How can we effectively tutor if our lived experiences with racism are continuously seen as an emotional unraveling or dismissed as anecdotal evidence rubbing up against "scientific" results?

WONDERFUL

I worked in writing centers for a little more than three years while getting my MA and PhD degrees from two separate institutions. I remember one specific session vividly because both the client with whom I worked and the reaction from other tutors who heard about the session left me incredulous. An international graduate student made an appointment with me to work on her dissertation. It was quite common for tutors to work with clients who were also graduate students.

I had no qualms about working with this student other than the fact that the dissertation was based in science and my field was Composition and Rhetoric. Although I had my own reservations, the student told me her dissertation was mostly complete, but because she was Chinese and her first language was not English, she wanted to ensure the grammar, cogency, cohesion, and coherence of her dissertation were satisfactory. I told her "no problem." Tutors worked with many international students at this writing center, so her request was quite common.

I began to have a sense of unease as she and I read her dissertation. Her dissertation was about sperm viability. The viability of sperm was not what caused my unease, though. As it was, my uneasiness was rooted in the premise on which this two-hundred-page dissertation was based: the idea that a woman, no matter her racial background, would have inferior children should she become impregnated by and consequently bear the offspring of a Black man. The premise was an argument begotten from the racist, sexist, and elitist history of eugenics.

Okeagu et al. (2010) notes, "Eugenics programs were inherently racist, elitist and sexist" (p. 993) and in North Carolina the eugenics movement dramatically targeted African Americans in the general population (p. 993). Pre-1960, more whites were sterilized than Blacks. However, in the 1960s, "when social workers had the authority to recommend sterilization, the number of African Americans who were sterilized increased dramatically to approximately 99%. The Biannual Eugenics Report for 1961 to 1968 stated that 99% of the operations were performed on women and 64% of the women were African Americans" (p. 994). I am never surprised at how the argument positing the Black race as an inferior continues. I was, however, surprised that this research and this argument for which a dissertation would be defended and a PhD would be given came from an international Chinese student, who upon entering the U.S. became just another racial minority considered inferior by the American eugenics movement.

I asked this student if she knew the premise of her entire dissertation was racist. She told me her dissertation was approved and that sperm viability was important to know in science, broadly, but in gynecology and genetics specifically. I mentioned to her she was not arguing sperm viability but arguing that the offspring of a man was immediately inferior due to his race. Although she could not tell me she was arguing a different point, I could not convince her that the point she made was insensitive, racist, and based in junk science—we moved on to grammar. Grammar was the out we both needed. Yet I was riddled with guilt.

This guilt was not because I told her that her dissertation was racist (it surely was), but because I could not fight this fight. I could not bear the emotional or intellectual labor. I found excuses for me and for her. I told myself that she worked hard on this nonsense, that it was not her fault, but the fault of her dissertation committee, and the fault of IRB for not catching it. I told myself I did all I could considering she might have filed a complaint.

When I discussed with other tutors who happened to be white what I had just endured, they dismissed my concern as an underappreciation for and a misunderstanding of science. (1) I have always appreciated the good bits of science that contributed to the advancement of the human race and (2) my lack of understanding of science extends only insofar as my desire not to make it my preferred academic discipline. These tutors told me that genetic diseases occur, some diseases are more likely to happen in one race versus another, and it's good to have this information for general knowledge and to combat it. Essentially, they made the exact same argument as my client with slightly better verbiage.

Much like my client, they willingly missed the point. They went further and silenced me when I tried to explain the point. BROUGHT UP THE POINT. This dissertation was not about hereditary diseases more likely to occur in African Americans (i.e., sickle cell anemia) than Caucasians. It was about the inferiority of Black male sperm. While both the client and these tutors were the ones changing the argument on the fly, it was I who was being unreasonable; I who was overly emotional; I who made an Asian international student think she was a racist, while negating the fact that I never called this Asian woman racist; I just called her argument racist—which it was. I was labeled the bad guy. Again. I was not surprised. I was disappointed.

This labeling as "the bad guy" is why I never pushed my clients to explain themselves further, and it's why I told these tutors that the next time she came in for a session, they could meet with her and encourage her racist premise, while massaging the egos of their racist ideology. What other option was there when my options were taken away because I was unheard?

What is the cost when one is asked to just grin and bear it? What is the price of being well trained in rhetoric when you can help those who believe you subhuman build "valid arguments" that deftly deconstruct your humanness, relegate you to subhuman, and reinforce ideologies that suggest that Brown, Black, and Indigenous people's function is to help serve and uphold white supremacist ideals?

BERNICE

The first night I worked with, let's call him Dave, I spent the hour listening to his story. It was a woeful account of gatekeepers. Dave was a nice young white man, a graduate of a flagship Midwestern university. Dave was a legacy scholarship student—one of his parents distinguished themselves at this flagship Midwestern university in some way and then crossed the border to the state next door. This made Dave eligible for 14K a year to cover nonresident tuition. After graduation, Dave's expectation of joining said flagship Midwestern film studies graduate program was dashed by gatekeepers. Dave was forced to take a job in middle management in a relatively middle-class workspace where he made a decent living. Dave was considering buying a house, but he wasn't ready to commit because Dave knew that he belonged in academia. He was going to be a film studies professor. The only reason he wasn't already in graduate school was those darned gatekeepers.

The first gatekeeper to rear their ugly head in the narrative was a literature professor who, kindly, explained to Dave that they could not, would not write a recommendation letter. They could not recommend Dave here or there or anywhere. This was deeply traumatic for Dave since his writing sample emerged from this class and the professor had been very helpful and nice, and they had spent a great deal of time talking about this paper, and Dave just didn't understand why the professor would not write a recommendation letter. And his other teachers hated him, especially the "minority" faculty. The second gatekeeper was my very own writing center and the way we privileged enrolled students. Since he no longer had a student ID number, he couldn't just make appointments, forcing him to depend on open walk-in times.

"That's why I'm here. Normally, I wouldn't work with you," said Dave. "But that woman told me that the writing center sites outside of the center work with everyone."

Those writing center sites were dorms, the Multicultural center, and other places that made it easier for students to access help with their writing. I spent three hours, twice a week, at a study stop that was open later than our writing center in hopes of encountering students who couldn't normally go to the center. Over the next year, I would spend at least two hours a week helping Dave craft a twenty-five-page writing sample and his graduate school materials. Often, I would spend more than two hours a week because Dave was careful to arrive early, so that he took up my first hour, and if there wasn't anyone waiting, he would argue for more time. Our policy was up to two hours a week with any given tutor. Enforcing the policy was at the tutor's discretion. Most of the time I enforced the policy, but there were plenty of times when he would return with "just one more question" or to ask if I could "read just one more page." On the nights I worked with Dave, I would go home, take a long shower—sometimes cry in the shower—and then crawl into bed. The next day I would often sleep late into the afternoon, too weary to drag myself out of bed to work on my own dissertation.

Before we go any further, dear reader, it's important to know four things.

1. I am a Latina. A Brown woman. My Indigenous roots are apparent in my body, my long hair, and my bone structure.

2. Dave is an open white nationalist who was writing a paper arguing that the United Nations was a terrorist group that intended to undermine American freedom and global power. His thesis was that the UN secretly financed anti-freedom-propaganda science fiction films in the 1950s to "soften" the American people to being "invaded" by "others." The films used aliens as other, but Dave made it clear that the UN meant to flood the U.S. with People of Color. He argued that the United Nations is an undercover cabal of communist minorities who want to destroy the white American's right to firearms and their right to prevent the "darkening" of our population. His main claims were that the United Nation's mandate to provide international protection to refugees and respect their human rights was intended to destroy American culture. He was trying to prove that films like "The Day the Earth Stood Still" were intended to soften the American people and make them more open to being globalized by the U.N. He argued the films could be traced back to anti-American propaganda creators through Darryl

Zanuck's relationships. Dave's work cited pages that were mostly Stormfront articles and memos from Darryl Zanuck. Although Dave's convictions and beliefs about People of Color were racist and violent, Dave was unfailingly polite, nice, and friendly.

3. I made it clear to Dave that I didn't agree with his argument, but that I could still help him. Then I helped Dave revise his paper so that his paper began with a candid reflection on his views of the U.N. and its role in producing anti-American propaganda and then moved to a thesis statement, which argued that "The Day the Earth Stood Still" could be defined as propaganda through the lens of the 1928 seminal text "Propaganda," by Edward L. Bernays. This was the compromise we came to after I explained to Dave that I disagreed with his thesis, I found his claims unsupported, and his sources unreliable. I explained that I was willing to help him craft an argument that would be taken seriously by academics and show him how to begin the text with a frank conversation of his bias.

4. Dave was accepted into a fully funded film studies graduate program in the South using the paper we worked on together. I still do not know how to feel about this.

These four things are important to our stories because none of these stories is really about a single director, client, or Dave. This isn't a story about how I was forced to work with Dave or how whiteliness—a term used by Marilyn Frye to describe the way white supremacy disguises itself as the best possible way of "thinking, speaking, and writing" so that white people can be both nice and racist—in my center forced me to work with Dave. No; I worked with Dave because I firmly believe that part of my anti-racist work is being fabulous and Brown in ways even the Daves of the world can't ignore. No matter how much he represses it, whenever he thinks of Mexicans, he will also see my face, hear my voice, and deep down he will know that he only got into grad school because a Mexican helped him write his paper. I consider this a part of my service to my community.

No—this is a story about what Rachel Elizabeth Cargle calls "Spiritual bypassing" which she describes as "The easiest way for white women to skirt around the realities of racism." Spiritual bypassing "is the use of spiritual practices and beliefs to avoid dealing with our painful feelings, unresolved wounds, and developmental needs. It is much more common than we might think and, in fact, is so pervasive as to go largely unnoticed, except in its more obvious extremes" (Masters). This happens when white women confronted with racial trauma fall back on unity, peace, kindness and love to force People of Color to recant their claim to trauma at the risk of being painted as mean or divisive. Spiritual bypassing was the rhetorical move used by Mitzi's director, Wonderful's client and peers, and my peers.

This is the story of the staff meeting where I tried to discuss how I felt about Dave getting into grad school, my worry that other Daves were inflicting this same kind of trauma on other tutors, and my desire do some training and policy crafting to actively protect student tutors from similar situations. This is the story of the white hot flash of anger, of the pain of my throat closing, and the humiliation of the tears I had to fight back when my white women "allies" negated my claim to trauma by suggesting that I wasn't being positive, that I was taking Dave's work "too personally" and that I should judge him on his behavior and not the worldview his paper displayed. According to my peers, I just needed to be thicker skinned because "we all" work with writers we don't agree with. I pointed out that very few of us work with people who see us as less than human and would like to see us and our families expelled from our country or exterminated.

That was when they pointed out that Dave never *said* any of those things; Dave, even though he had opinions I disagreed with, had always been *nice* to me. I just needed to focus on what really mattered—helping the client. In a matter of minutes, these white women had redefined my experience—the fact that I had spent at least two hours a week helping a man who embodied a racist worldview write a paper that proclaimed people like me were less than human and undeserving of human rights—into nothing more than my overreacting to the opinion of a perfectly nice guy.

Our center director said little, so little in fact that I don't remember what she said or if she said anything. I just remember realizing, in that moment, how overwhelmingly white the center had become over her time as director, and how, aside from our international receptionist, I was one of very few (maybe the only) Tutor of Color. I do remember a white woman accomplice trying to gently, kindly, and lovingly explain to the rest of the room that People of Color experience trauma when forced to share space with people who would like to see us and our loved ones eradicated from the fabric of our society—but then getting bogged down in white tears and proclamations of "not being racist." They effectively derailed the conversation, re-centered it on how white people felt, and shut me down. Looking back, I'm a little ashamed for letting it happen. I could have pushed harder, could have insisted on being heard, but I didn't have the emotional energy. Things had changed when our leadership changed. The new director, a woman of color, had her hands full fighting for the center in general. She didn't have the same kind of power as our former director, a tenure track professor who specialized in anti-racism work, and she was just finishing out her first year.

Regardless of how much she wanted to be an ally, she also lacked the resources she needed. In that environment, whiteliness just crept into the space and took root. I knew walking out of that meeting that I was done in our writing center. I finished my semester and never returned.

Spiritual bypassing, ignoring the racial harm and trauma committed against a person of color by falling back on "reheated wisdom[s]" like "Don't take it personally" (Masters) is a staple of white feminism and one that can quickly take root in the writing center environment. Because centers strive to be student-centered and to help as many writers as possible, it is easy for spiritual bypassing to become part of the culture of the center. This creates situations like Mitzi's, where she is labeled the problem by her peers, and her director focuses only on how Mitzi can change instead of how the center can change. Spiritual bypassing creates environments where tutors are not supported in calling out blatant racism when it shows up in student papers, and if they do speak up, they are once again cast as the problem.

Spiritual bypassing is particularly insidious and hard to combat because it allows white women to fall back on ideals of "light and love and kindness," to discount and disregard real accounts of pain and trauma by People of Color. Instead of dealing with the problem or even acknowledging it, we are offered some form of trite "positivity culture" that reinforces the idea that we, the People of Color, are really the problem because we are not "being positive" or "putting into the world what we want to get out of the world." Since positivity, being writer-centered, and focusing on helping others is the culture of the center, it's nearly impossible for tutors of color to name, call out, or speak up against spiritual bypassing without encountering enormous pushback.

The danger of spiritual bypassing in any ecology, but especially in an environment like the writing center, where the overall goal is to be kind and helpful, is that spiritual bypassing "has so deeply and thoroughly infiltrated our culture that it has become all but normalized . . . [it] fits almost seamlessly into our collective habit of turning away from what is painful, as a kind of higher analgesic with seemingly minimal side effects. It is a spiritualized strategy not only for avoiding pain but also for *legitimizing* such avoidance, in ways ranging from the blatantly obvious to the extremely subtle" (Masters). Moreover, when a person of color is immersed in a writing center where a "positivity culture" that legitimizes avoidance of their trauma and experiences has become the norm, it makes the center a racist and toxic space. "Too often, positive thinking seems to belong to people in positions of privilege; and it is used to erase the experience of others who are less privileged. . . . Positive thinking, taken to an extreme is pathological; it becomes a fear of any unwanted feeling . . . emotion, subject, or problem" (Kleppinger). Positive thinking is not a remedy for racism; niceness will not save us; and there is no way to avoid taking racism personal—it is deeply personal. Allowing positive thinking to become the foundation of a writing center culture without examining it critically creates an environment that invites spiritual bypassing to become the norm.

REFERENCES

Cargle, R. E. (2019, May 28). When feminism is white supremacy in heels. Retrieved from http://www.harpersbazaar.com/culture/politics/a22717725/what-is-toxic-white -feminism/.

Frye, M. (1992). *Willful Virgin: Essays in Feminism, 1976–1992*. Freedom, CA: Crossing Press.

Kleppinger, U. (2019, February 10). The cult of oppressive positivity. Retrieved from http://www.pregamemagazine.com/cult-oppressive-positivity/.

Masters, R. A. (2013). Spiritual bypassing. Retrieved from http://www.robertmasters.com/ 2013/04/29/spiritual-bypassing/.

Okeagu, J. E., et al. (2010). The dialectics and social impact of the American eugenics movement on African Americans. Scarborough: National Association of African American Studies.

SECTION THREE

Essaying White Anti-Racism

8

RESISTING WHITE, PATRIARCHAL EMOTIONAL LABOR WITHIN THE WRITING CENTER

Nicole I. Caswell

"I performed whiteness (which to me meant to be emotionally absent from my teaching and learning so that people would not have to see my color) to the best of my ability for my students, peers, and professors, which I'll admit, is not too hard considering I do not have a colored accent and my skin color, well, is light enough to make people wonder 'what I am.'"

(Faison & Treviño, 2017)

In "Race, retention, language and literacy: The hidden curriculum of the writing center," Faison and Treviño (2017) narrate multiple moments where they were required to engage in emotional labor. Through their stories of emotional labor, they challenge the narrative of writing centers as cozy homes (Grutsch McKinney, 2013) where all are welcomed and supported. Faison and Treviño demonstrate that writing centers are cozy homes for *some*. Welcoming for *some*. Supportive for *some*. At least in the writing center I direct, and the ones Faison and Treviño worked in—and I'd bet many other writing centers—that *some* is the white, middle-class, heteronormative writer. Writing centers are built upon the power and privilege of white heteronormativity. When thinking about writing centers as sites of power and privilege, I cannot help but think of the people and emotions that circulate within the site. While physical walls and furniture create tangible boundaries to define the space, the individuals within the space and the emotions that circulate within the space create an affective economy that invites, rejects, celebrates, and/ or harms individuals who try to enter the writing center. Writing centers are rich with affective economies that demand and shape directors' and consultants' emotional labor.

https://doi.org/10.7330/9781646421534.c008

Writing center scholars recognize that emotion and emotional labor is woven into the work of consultants (Agostinelli, Poch, & Santoro, 2000; Sherwood, 1995) and directors (Caswell, Grutsch McKinney, & Jackson, 2016), but writing center scholars have not thought much about the ways our emotions also perpetuate a white, middle-class, patriarchal affective economy that furthers the whiteness of writing centers through emotional power and privilege. In this chapter, I explore the affective economies of writing centers and the emotional labor of writing center directors. This chapter looks at how emotions function at two levels within the writing center: affective economies and emotional labor. These two levels share emotion in reciprocal ways. The affective economies construct spaces that invite writing center directors to engage in emotional labor, and directors' emotional labor reinforces or challenges the affective economies of the space. Affective economies consider how emotion circulates outside of individuals, whereas emotional labor considers how emotions work within bodies. This chapter begins by defining affective economies through an extended example of standard academic English and then moves into a discussion of emotional labor. Through the discussion of emotional labor, I consider the role of writing center directors' emotional labor in resisting a patriarchal affective economy and instead creating a more socially just, inclusive writing center space. In particular, as writing center scholars continue to investigate emotional labor as a framework for understanding writing center work, I argue that white[1] writing center directors must actively resist emotional labor as a new framework for re-inscribing white bodies, behaviors, and emotions onto other bodies as *the* normalized practices and experiences of writing center director work. In other words, emotional labor must be viewed as a complex, multidirectional framework that ensures representation of non-white bodies, behaviors, and emotions as central to our understanding of emotional labor. This chapter concludes with ways in which white writing center directors can intervene in the patriarchal affective economies flourishing in writing centers.

Before discussing affective economies though, I want to be transparent about the ways I fit into the world. I am particularly cognizant of my positionality while writing this chapter and how my thinking has been shaped by what I am asking us to resist. Though I am committed to social justice work in the writing center and academy, the lines of privilege intersect my identity at multiple points and shape and constrain

---

1. This chapter approaches white women as a socially and politically recognized group with particular race-given privileges, freedoms, and liberties (Frye, 1983).

my commitment. At an institutional level, I am a white tenured associate professor and writing center director. Within the field, I am part of
the dominant demographics as a white woman writing center director.
Culturally, I identify with the dominant markers as a heterosexual, white,
U.S. citizen. All of these privileges grant me particular protections. I
cannot take these markers off, and the power that comes with these
markers is an elusive force that even with the best of intentions, I fall
victim to. To that end, I also want to be transparent that I am focusing
on white writing center directors in this chapter not simply because I am
one or they make up the majority of writing center director positions,
but because "white women are *almost* white men, [and] being white, at
least, and sometimes more-or-less honorary men, we can cling to a hope
of true membership in the dominant and powerful group, and if our
focus is thus locked on them by this futile hope, we can be stuck in our
ignorance and theirs all our lives" (Frye, 1983). We white women writing
center directors have work to do.

AFFECTIVE ECONOMIES IN THE WRITING CENTER

According to Ahmed (2004), emotions do not reside within individuals. Instead, emotions circulate between bodies and surfaces, sticking to
some and leaving residual traces to be picked up again. Micciche (2007)
builds on Ahmed's work, arguing we do emotion, and that emotions do
not happen to us. Micciche believes emotions help us construct or enact
behaviors, and we perform emotions for particular purposes. Ahmed
and Micciche are both invested in how "emotions *involve* subjects and
objects, but without residing positively within them" (Ahmed, 2004,
p. 119). Through a queer, feminist, cultural understanding of emotion,
individuals do not inherently have emotions in the sense of how we
define happiness, anger, or fear; and individuals are not made to feel
particular ways by objects. While individuals have the same biological
and chemical processes when an emotion has been triggered[2], the recognition and naming of that process is a social, cultural act. Individuals
respond to their emotions based on how they have been socially and
culturally conditioned to do so. Thus, emotions mediate the ways we
experience the world.

Affective economies, then, refer to the ways emotions travel and stick
to bodies and objects. In an affective economy, emotions become capital

2. For more information on the biological, neurological, social, and cultural definitions
   of emotion, see Damasio, 1999; Scherer, 2000; Milton, 2007; and Wetherell, 2012.

commodified through their circulation. We might see an increase in affective value the more some bodies, signs, and objects circulate. Affective economies are social, material, and psychic, and "it is the failure of emotions to be located in a body, object, or figures that allows emotions to (re)produce or generate the effects that they do" (Ahmed, 2004, p. 124). Within the writing center, affective economies perpetuate the white, middle-class, patriarchal ideologies by circulating emotion in ways that implicitly shape writing center practices. For example, the writing center-as-a-cozy-home metaphor carries with it the emotional traces of white, middle-class homes. The notion that including a coffee pot and couch will cultivate ease among writers is grounded in the idea that these objects carry emotional effects. Rubrics and other assessment measures within writing centers also carry emotional traces of power and privilege that manifest in multiple emotional experiences for those carrying out assessment or those subjected to assessment. Writing centers' abilities to shape or shake these emotional traces depends on the ways writing centers reproduce or disengage the emotional capital embedded in bodies, signs, and objects.

As one example of an affective economy, we might turn to the emotional attachments and meanings involved in Standard Academic English (SAE) within writing centers. Writing centers' history with SAE has left residual emotional traces that continues to generate effects in writing centers today. If we think about how writing centers evolved as spaces to remediate bodies not able to perform SAE in the classroom, we can consider the complex affective value of SAE over time. Writing in SAE was (still is) the mark of the privileged (Greenfield, 2011). When writing centers emerged in colleges across the country, they evolved as sites to cure writing ailments—or help writers write like white people. Particular bodies (non-white, non-upper-middle class) were repeatedly marked as deficient and the presence of these bodies in the classroom became read as threats to the academy. These bodies were then sent to the writing center to later emerge as sounding white. As Greenfield (2011) reminds us, "By suggesting that 'Standard English' exists as a language variety, rather than acknowledging that 'Standard English' is, by definition, the conglomeration of all privileged white speech, we set up a hypothetical ideal for all people which, for people of color, can never in reality be attained" (pp. 57–58). Faculty continue to leave emotional traces through their coded, racist narratives of students' writing as "not being professional enough" or students "write like they talk." These narratives leave behind affective markers on the students and writing center because the absence of SAE threatens the academy and challenges those in power. Writers end up either belonging to the academy—or they don't. The absence of SAE constructs emotions of fear, failure, and repulsion that circulate within the writing center and academy. The repetition of needing to perform SAE has placed affective value on particular bodies so that, as soon as they walk into writing center spaces, consultants unconsciously read their bodies as failures or sessions that'll take more work.

In sessions focused on writing in SAE, consultants perform their jobs based on how they read the affective economy. Consultants might try to "sell" and "help others" learn SAE because they are so ingrained in the system and their use of SAE might be part of the reason they applied to work in the writing center. When working with non-SAE writing, consultants might adapt a savior-approach to help the writer sound white under the guise of wanting that writer to be successful. Or, they might view the session as a time to work on the basics of writing and only focus on surface-level concerns. Or, a consultant might resist the idea that SAE is the only way to write and instead help a writer rhetorically respond to their assignment. However a consultant might approach the situation, that approach has been mediated by the emotions circulating in the space and among the bodies present (and, of course, by the ways the director has articulated the mission of the writing center and engaged consultants in professional development). Within sessions and while writers are writing, emotions continue to circulate by reminding writers they remain on the periphery of the academy by not using SAE and that, without SAE, they'll never "get the A." The academy creates a lived-sense of the power of SAE and that power is perpetuated through an affective economy.

Though very prevalent and powerful, SAE is only one narrative enacted through an affective economy that maintains the power of the academic white, middle-class, patriarchal ideologies. By continuing to align with SAE, writing centers have restricted the mobility of writers who do not identify with SAE. Writing centers that continue to align with SAE are participating in an inherently racist affective economy. Affective economies continue to perpetuate privileged, normalized narratives in institutional spaces in ways individuals don't necessarily recognize. Thus, affective economies can subvert writing centers' work toward social justice by subconsciously reinscribing the power and privilege firmly entrenched in our centers, pedagogies, and practices. To work toward social justice, writing centers must confront the various affective economies in our spaces and resist the narrative that academic mobility is tied to SAE.

EMOTIONAL LABOR WITHIN AFFECTIVE ECONOMIES

Just as consultants read and contribute to the affective economy of the writing center, writing center directors also contribute, but seem to play a more prominent role in shaping the affective economies. Like Micciche suggests, writing center directors perform emotions for particular purposes, and these purposes can shape, constrain, and/or resist different affective economies. Emotional labor, one particular emotional performance for writing center directors, might happen unconsciously rather than consciously. In *The Working Lives of New Writing Center Directors*, Caswell, Grutsch McKinney, and Jackson (2016) define emotional labor as relational work that writing center directors engage in to make the rest of their job (everyday and disciplinary labor) run smoothly. Emotional labor was not only experiencing an emotion, but having their emotion tied to an activity or task (and, within an affective economy framework, I'd extend that to include bodies as well). Emotional labor was work writing center directors wanted to do or felt they had to do so their other tasks went more smoothly. Emotional labor is often invisible, creditless work, but necessary to run a writing center. Additionally, emotional labor as a construct is not located in the director or in the writing center (though performed and embodied by the individual), but within the white institutional space of the academy. We know that certain emotional behaviors are privileged as white; and in the academy, we are expected to perform in the privileged white way.

For sociologist Arlie Hochschild (1983), emotional labor is done in service to the profession—individuals engage in emotional labor in exchange for pay. Focusing mostly on service positions, such as flight attendants, individuals must suppress themselves into order to adopt a particular emotional role given to them by the industry. Flight attendants, for example, must be friendly, kind, and always helpful. Even when faced with rude, racist flyers, flight attendants must manage their emotions to appear helpful and kind. Emotional labor ends up being either a performance of normalized emotion behaviors or a performance of making others feel a particular way. Hochschild's emotional labor theory informs the emotional labor Caswell, Grutsch McKinney, and Jackson detail for new writing center directors, but Caswell et al. also expand the definition of emotional labor to include the relational work individuals do to connect with other individuals, thus pulling in the more positive experiences of emotional labor for writing center directors. This is not to say the suppressing of self doesn't happen to writing center directors, but that the relational work does not ask all directors to adopt the same industry role. Instead, writing center directors end up following the unwritten social script to determine what is acceptable or not acceptable within the academic site of the writing center.

This unwritten social script constructs feeling rules individuals must follow when displaying emotions in spaces. Feeling rules are delineated based on gender, race, social class, and other identity markers, and they establish the normative expressions of emotion allowed. For example, there's no crying in baseball, but funerals and weddings are acceptable places to cry—for *some*. It is important to note that the social script of feeling rules shifts depending on the body. As Evans (2013) writes, gender and race become markers for not whether individuals can engage in emotional labor, but how much emotional labor they must ceaselessly navigate to complete their jobs. All writing center directors engage in emotional labor—no one seems immune from it. But, while engaging in emotional labor transcends identity markers, our experiences of emotional labor are entangled with our identities. In the larger emotional labor scholarship, there has been limited research on the racialized aspect of emotional labor. We can see this in writing center studies, too. Though Geller et al. in *The Everyday Writing Center* did not use the term *emotional labor*, implicitly they established there is no way to discuss race without simultaneously discussing emotional labor. For example, they state "there is no way to talk about race without also talking about hopes, fears, pain and pride" (p. 90). Emotional labor is firmly embedded within the chapter "Everyday Racism." Readers can imagine the emotional labor Krista managed as an African American tutor who was constantly questioned by her fellow tutors about whether she needed an appointment. Emotional labor is also embedded within writing center scholarship on racial identities (Condon, 2007; Diab, Godbee, & Simpkins, 2012; Faison & Treviño, 2017; Greenfield & Rowan, 2011), but we have not yet named the stories and experiences *as* examples of emotional labor.

Evans (2013) builds on Hochschild's research by incorporating race in her study on the emotional labor of African Americans within the airline industry. Evans advocates for the inclusion of context within an emotional labor framework positing that context shapes the emotional labor of employees and that "emotional labor and the process through which it operates cannot be separated from the larger structural conditions and ideologies in which it is required" (p. 11). Much of emotional labor becomes codified into positions by those who occupy the role. In writing centers, we can imagine that the emotional work of writing center directors becomes normalized through the work of white women writing center directors. The behaviors, performances, and expectations of writing center directors are those that white writing center directors have been doing. Conscious or not, the choices white women make in writing center work shape the narrative of what is expected of other writing center directors and the emotional roles writing center directors are permitted to perform. The choices white women directors make and the reactions they have can (and do and have) create(d) real consequences for other directors.

Being in leadership roles, women writing center directors also navigate an emotional tightrope of being perceived as either too competent (masculine) or too nice (feminine) (Grigoryan, 2017). Grigoryan (2017) reflects on how white women must not veer too far in either direction as to not perform their gendered expectations, while also always being nurturing, understanding, and cheerful. To be successful in the academy, white women must be likeable, competent, and feminine. And, when white women writing center directors submit to these gender rules and "play the (sexist) game" for their own success, they establish the acceptable behaviors, performances, and expectations for all directors. Similar to other professions, the emotional displays allowed by and for white women are not appropriate when Black women display them. Evans writes "even when feelings are normative, they are more normative within specific identity characteristics and are not equally applied, suggesting that workers of color must simultaneously engage organizational rules of feeling and emotional labor as well as those group-specific rules of feeling and labor" (p. 5). This duality of emotional labor places undue burden on directors of color that is not captured within our current scholarship of emotional labor. Durr and Harvey Wingfield (2011) write "For black women workers, attempting to perform the appropriate emotional labor while simultaneously conforming to etiquette norms creates specific issues that may not be present for other race/gender groups" (p. 568). Directors of color must conform their emotional labor to that of white directors; only, directors of color are not socially and culturally permitted to perform white emotional labor and thus are forced to engage in multifaceted layers of emotional labor that white directors do not. For example, displays of anger, when warranted, are OK for white women directors, but Black women directors cannot display anger without falling into the stereotypical "angry Black woman" trope. It should be no surprise professors and directors of color experience a disproportionate level of emotional labor (Gay, 2014; Green, 2018), but writing center studies has limited research on micro/macro-aggression, racial battle fatigue, and institutionalized patriarchal structures through an emotional labor lens. We need more research and stories to better understand racialized emotional labor and how to support professors and directors of color in ways that do not ask them to seek our support.

For writing centers, layering context onto emotional labor seems like one way to incorporate the emotional lived experiences of writing center directors into our core understanding of what emotional labor is for writing center directors. Another layer white women writing center directors must acknowledge is how our experiences and performances of emotional labor (particularly emotional management) establishes normalized practices for writing center directors that non-white bodies can and cannot perform. When studying and discussing the emotional labor of writing center directors, we must actively engage in conversations and experiences of what directors of color experience even if white directors do not comprehend such experiences. The additional emotional labor directors of color experience should be central to our understanding of how directors build relationships and make sense of the writing center space. Emotional labor should not be bracketed as experienced by white directors with additional burden on directors of color; instead, we need a framework that is robust enough to account for the multiplicity of ways emotional labor can be experienced. For writing center directors, emotional labor is a complex navigation of social identity politics[3] necessary to perform the relational work of writing centers. Emotional labor can be internally and externally experienced, but it is shaped by the affective economies of the writing center and larger academic institution.

CONCLUSION

Influenced by the larger institutional structure of education, the writing center serves as a micro-space of cultural, political, and institutional power (Grimm, 1999) that is experienced through affective economies and emotional labor. Emotions mediate the everyday and disciplinary labor of writing center work through the two layers of affective economies and emotional labor. Affective economies and emotional labor work together to perpetuate the power and privilege of institutional structures. To create a more socially just, inclusive writing center space, writing center directors must intervene and actively resist the normative emotional labor and affective economy narratives.

---

3. Though this chapter primarily focuses on the intersection of race and gender as it applies to white women's emotional labor, I also recognize that a robust emotional labor definition must attend to the intersectional work of social identity politics.

To cultivate affective economies that resist the white, middle-class, patriarchal institution, white women writing center directors need to constantly listen, reflect, and act. White women writing center directors can

- quit perpetuating the false narrative of Standard Academic English as a means of writerly success and name it as the privileged, white voice (Greenfield, 2011).
- subscribe to socially just and inclusive pedagogies and writing center practices.
- examine the physical writing center space to understand the ideologies and values embedded in the posters, books, furniture, and other everyday objects.
- get comfortable with not being liked by resisting scripted gender roles. When white women behave outside stereotypical gender norms, they create space to challenge assumed feeling rules (Grigoryan, 2017).
- listen to the faculty, staff, and students of color on our campuses and **act** on their suggestions for support.
- recognize that silence does not equal acceptance or agreement from directors and consultants of color. For their emotional protection, directors and consultants of color might not engage in racist, oppressive conversations or behaviors (Evans & Moore, 2015).
- incorporate context and social identity politics when researching emotional labor.

For white women writing center directors, affective economies and emotional labor allow us to move more freely in the space, dipping in and out of our privilege when we see fit. White writing center directors need to allow for writing center spaces to change by advocating for the construction of new feeling rules that incorporate the lived experiences of directors of color. White writing center directors need to orient and align our emotional bodies with others. We must not simply speak up or advocate, but instead promote an affective economy that doesn't create emotional boundaries for directors of color to navigate on top of the rest of their work.

REFERENCES

Agostinelli, C., Poch, H., & Santoro, E. (2000). Tutoring in emotionally charged session. In B. Rafoth (Ed.), *A Tutor's Guide: Helping Writers One to One* (pp. 34–41). Heinemann.

Ahmed, S. (2004). Affective Economies. *Social Text* 79.22 (2), 117–139.

Caswell, N., Grutsch McKinney, J., & Jackson, R. (2016). *The Working Lives of New Writing Center Directors.* Utah State University Press.

Condon, F. (2007). Beyond the known: Writing centers and the work of anti-racism. *The Writing Center Journal,* 27(2), 19–38.

Damasio, A. (1999). *The Feeling of What Happens.* Harvest Books.

Daufin, E.-K. (2017). The problem with the phrase "women and minorities": Racism and sexism intersectionality for black women faculty. In K. Cole & H. Hassel (Eds.), *Surviving Sexism in Academia: Strategies for Feminist Leadership.* (pp. 57–67). Routledge.

Diab, R., Godbee, B., Ferrel, T., & Simpkins, N. (2012). A multi-dimensional pedagogy for racial justice in writing centers. *Praxis: A Writing Center Journal, 10*(1). http://www.praxisuwc.com/diab-godbee-ferrell-simpkins-101/

Durr, M. & Harvey Wingfield, A. M. (2011). Keep your "n" in check: African American women and the interactive effects of etiquette and emotional labor. *Critical Sociology, 37*(5), 557–571.

Evans, L. (2013). *Cabin Pressure: African American Pilots, Flight Attendants, and Emotional Labor.* Rowman & Littlefield Publishers.

Evans, L. & Moore, W. L. (2015). Impossible burdens: White institutions, emotional labor, and micro-resistance. *Social Problems, 62*, 439–454.

Fasion, W. & Treviño, A. (2017). Race, retention, language, and literacy: The hidden curriculum of the writing center. *The Peer Review, 1*(2). http://thepeerreview-iwca.org/issues/braver-spaces/race-retention-language-and-literacy-the-hidden-curriculum-of-the-writing-center/

Frye, M. (1983). On being white. *The Politics of Reality: Essays in Feminist Theory.* (pp. 110–127). Crossing Press.

Frye, M. (1992). White woman feminist 1983–1992. In *Wilful Virgin: Essays in Feminism, 1976–1992.* (pp. 147–169). Crossing Press.

Gay, R. (2014). *Bad Feminist Essays.* Harper Perennial.

Geller, A., Eodice, M., Condon, F., Carroll, M., Boquet, E. (2007). *The Everyday Writing Center.* Utah State University Press.

Green, N. (2018). Moving beyond alright: And the emotional toll of this, my life matters too, in the writing center work. *The Writing Center Journal, 37*(1), 15–34.

Greenfield, L. (2011). The 'standard English' fairy tale. In L. Greenfield & K. Rowan (Eds.) *Writing Centers and the New Racism: A Call for Sustainable Dialogue and Change.* (pp. 33–60) Utah State University Press.

Greenfield, L. & Rowan, K., eds. (2011). *Writing Centers and the New Racism: A Call for Sustainable Dialogue and Change.* Utah State University Press.

Grigoryan, A. (2017). You are too blunt, too ambitious, too confident. In K. Cole & H. Hassel (Eds.), *Surviving Sexism in Academia: Strategies for Feminist Leadership.* (pp. 243–249). Routledge.

Grimm, N. (1999) *Good Intentions: Writing Center Work for Postmodern Times.* Heinemann.

Grutsch McKinney, J. (2013). *Peripheral Visions for Writing Centers.* Utah State University Press.

Hochschild A. R. (1983). *The Managed Heart: The Commercialization of Human Feeling.* University of California Press.

Micciche, L. (2007). *Doing Emotion: Rhetoric, Writing, Teaching.* Boynton/Cook Publishers.

Milton, K. (2007). Emotion (or life, the universe, everything). In H. Wulff (Ed.), *The Emotions: A Cultural Reader* (pp. 61–76). Berg.

Scherer, K. (2000). Emotion. In M. Hewstone and W. Stroebe (Eds.), *Introduction to Social Psychology: A European Perspective,* (3rd ed., pp. 151–91). Blackwell.

Sherwood, S. (1995). The dark side of the helping personality: Student dependency and the potential for tutor burnout. In Stay B., Murphy, C., & Hobson, E. (Eds.), *Writing Center Perspectives* (pp. 63–70). National Writing Centers Association Press.

Wetherell, M. (2012). *Affect and Emotion: A New Social Science Understanding.* SAGE.

9

A LONG PATH TO *SEMI*-WOKE

Jill Reglin

When approached to submit a chapter to this collection, my first thought was: *I am not qualified.* My disclaimers about *why* were elaborate. I recoiled at the thought of investigating my ideology in public, at exposing that I am not yet "woke." As I put the finishing touches on the final draft of this contribution, I feel largely the same. The benevolence of white womanhood has allowed me until now to guard against exposing myself as uninformed, or worse yet, as subscribing to an ideology of color-blind racism. I occupy the safe and powerful position of the white, middle-aged, cisgendered, middle-class, mid-career academic who is permitted to adopt the stance that "Everything's-OK-Everybody's-OK -I-get-how-you-feel" without being routinely asked, "Really? *Do you?*" White, middle-class women survive easily through social cooperation because we are members of the majority and semi-marginalized all at once. It is easy to smile and nod, to adopt the persona of the "good listener," to hide behind what we don't understand and to hope that nobody notices because unless we choose to expose ourselves, *nobody really does.*

In order to contribute to this collection, I had to choose to do just that—to willingly and publicly expose the limits of my critical self-examination, to push myself beyond the fear of revealing my own ignorance. I had to acknowledge that the ideology of color-blind racism as described by scholars like Bonilla-Silva (2018) had shaped and continues to shape how I "articulate [my] views (by relying on the frames of the ideology), present [my] ideas (by using the style of the ideology), and interpret interactions with people of color (by sharing the racial stories of the ideology)" (p. 142). I had to ask the editors of this collection, my longtime colleagues and friends, Wonderful Faison and Frankie Condon, what they had heard me say and what they had seen me do that caused them to encourage my submission in the first place—and I had to listen and trust what they told me. In reviewing their

https://doi.org/10.7330/9781646421534.c009

feedback on multiple drafts, I was forced to admit to them over and over, "I don't understand what you are suggesting here. I don't know what this means." Their clarification caused me to peel back the layers of my whiteness, and that, in itself, was a growth experience for me.

In the end, I don't deserve a gold star for bravery. The comforting *and disheartening* fact is this: When this chapter goes to print, no matter the critique it might receive, I can retreat into my glass cubicle to carry on in my work with little fear of serious repercussion. This is the privilege I am afforded up front. O'Brien (2001), in *Whites Confront Racism: Antiracists and Their Paths to Action*, uses the term "privileged resistance" to describe a "greater range of strategies white antiracists can use because of white privilege" (p. 74) and goes on to say whites are "less likely to suffer repercussions and social stigma for speaking out about racism" (p. 83). Though I do not consider writing this essay an act of resistance, I do acknowledge and accept that I enter the conversation with a safety net in place. But I also recognize that the need is critical for white women to talk out loud about social and racial injustice, as far as we are able to understand it. And so, I elect to participate.

A white, female colleague and I were exchanging stories about a student we had both taught and found to be especially challenging. I lamented to my colleague, "I tried everything I could think of to get through to her." "Maybe there's just something about us as *white women* . . . the way we look or talk . . . or *something*," my colleague trailed off as she rounded the corner back to her office. I believed she was right, though there would have been a time when I dismissed her and refused to accept it was *us*, as teachers, not *them*, as students. White benevolence blinds us from seeing what students of color, of disadvantage, and of non-privilege see. It blinds us from seeing how we participate in the preservation of oppression. In *White Women, Race Matters: The Social Construction of Whiteness*, Frankenberg (1993) observes that ". . . white women's lives are affected by racism, but frequently in ways that simultaneously conceal or normalize race privilege from the standpoint of its beneficiaries" (p. 161). Though I will never experience what my marginalized students experience, I have learned to listen and to trust that what they are sharing is representative of what they have seen and lived. It has taken me a while even to get this far.

Awareness began with small fissures in my world view caused by very personal stories a few of my Black colleagues chose to share with me. I can say with some amount of certainty that I was not the kind of person my colleagues of color would have shared their stories with when I first began my career in academia. O'Brien (2001) and the anti-racists interviewed in *Whites Confront Racism* stress that it is essential for whites to practice humility in order to gain the acceptance of people of color (p. 109). One interviewee specifically "made the point that authentic relationships with people of color serve the function of holding whites accountable to the communities they claim to be helping" (p. 124). I cannot say I was practicing deliberate humility when my colleagues began talking to me, that I was consciously aware of seeking "authentic relationships" with people of color, or that I was focused on helping them as individuals or members of our academic community. But I was and remain grateful that they somehow trusted me enough to tell me their stories. Bonilla-Silva (2018) discusses the risks involved for my colleagues of color in choosing to share these stories with me. The choice to share experiences or "telling truths to friends usually hurts both parties" (p. 245). The sharing began nevertheless with a Black man who taught English in my department. Every time he accepted a substitute teaching assignment at one of our rural, branch campuses in the heart of Michigan KKK country, he was stopped by security. Every single time they asked if they could help him with something and then followed him to his classroom after he said he was a professor—just to be sure he wasn't making it up. He had started wearing a suit when he went there, though it did little to stop the harassment he felt. I had been to that campus, myself, to observe other teachers and offer workshops. I walked in like I belonged there, knowing nobody, and I was greeted with a simple hello and left alone to proceed down the hallway without much notice. The fact that I was a member of the white majority allowed me to fly under the radar, and the fact that I looked every bit the part of a woman contributed to my nonthreatening presence. I would have never thought about this before my colleague chose to share his counternarrative with me.

A young Black woman finishing her Master's degree at the nearby university did a teaching internship with me. She had grown up in a mostly Black, mostly poor city not too far from my own hometown and was the first person in her family to go to college, which was not necessarily surprising to me. What was new to me about her story was how much *dis*couragement she had received from her own high school classmates, brothers, parents, and even teachers when she said she wanted to (1) graduate and (2) attend a university. Her family made fun of her for how much time she spent engaged in study; her peers knocked books out of her hands as she tried to read on the school bus, asking, "Why do you wanna be white?" In the high school I had attended, thirty miles away in the same county, it was expected that my classmates and

I were going to college. This was our default mode. The discussion my friends and I had with our parents focused only on *where*, not *if*. We were taught that, after all, we were supposed to be educated. Education would lead to a safe and secure future. My student teacher's friends and family feared what would happen when she was educated into the white middle-class thinking that dominates higher education. Black scholars like hooks (2000) warn us that we cannot separate discussions about race from discussions about class: "Clearly, just when we should all be paying attention to class, using race and gender to understand and explain its new dimensions, society, even our government, says let's talk about race and racial injustice. It is impossible to talk meaningfully about ending racism without talking about class. Let us not be duped." A mere thirty geographic miles separated where I grew up from where my student teacher had been raised. But the two communities were a cultural world apart in terms of both race and class.

Though my family wasn't wealthy, we were what my parents described as "comfortably middle-class." Both of my parents had bachelor's degrees. I was the fourth generation to go to college on my mom's side of the family. My father was a successful business owner, and my mom had taught elementary school for a number of years before leaving the profession to become the full-time stay-at-home mom of an only child. She, too, later owned a small business. My preservice teacher grew up in a poor neighborhood within a working-class community in a household where education was suspect and close family members were absent or in prison or struggling to put food on the table. I would guess the characteristics of her family could be traced back for generations, just as my family of educated business owners went back as far as I knew. My family's racial and class history, combined, created opportunities, where hers created obstacles.

The experiences of my colleagues in comparison to my own caused me to begin observing interactions with students who visited the writing center differently. One day, a Black man, probably in his early twenties, came through the door, walked past the front counter and began meandering around our student work area. Our front counter staff member asked him repeatedly if she could help him with something. He repeated in response, "I'm a student here." Though the staff member's motive was to find out what the student needed from the writing center, and though the student was addressed in the same manner anyone else would have been, his perception was that he fell under some sort of suspicion because of who he was and where he was. In anger, he finally repeated once again that he was a student and shouted that he had as much of a right to be in the space as any other student. He stormed out the door, stating that he was going to complain to someone. To the staff member, this was about trying to find out what the young man (who she assumed was a student from the start) needed from us. To the student, it was about someone questioning his belonging, much like it probably was for my Black colleague who showed up to substitute teach at our rural branch campus.

I can attribute a lot of my early awareness to my relationship with one student. Mandie took pre-college composition with me, and though she attended every day, she sat in the front row with a scowl on her face and rarely did her work. She didn't want to talk to anybody—especially me, it seemed. Her grade, not surprisingly, was suffering. Every time I collected homework, and she didn't have hers, I would say things like, "Mandie, you've gotta start getting your stuff in." When the first essay was due, Mandie turned in a revised draft that was two paragraphs long, and I had no idea where one sentence ended and the next began. She had told me on the first day of class that she was a pre-nursing student. I gave her a zero on her essay—because how could I not? Mandie began to approach me after class, which she had never done before. But one of her classmates, a bouncy, young, high-achieving white guy, slipped in between us to ask a question, and when I looked up, Mandie was halfway out the door. I followed her down the hall, urging her to stay because we "really need to talk." She had another class, she said. I asked her to come to my office hour later. "Whatever, I'll try," was all she said, as she turned toward me before getting into an elevator. For some reason, I looked at Mandie's face in that moment and saw something I had not seen before. Through the façade of that ever-present scowl, her face told me, "I know you're singling me out, and I know why." My focus up until that moment had been on Mandie's self-sabotaging student behaviors, not on myself and what I might be doing to perpetuate that behavior. Suddenly I wondered how many other white, female teachers, over the course of her education, had talked to her the way I did, had gotten on her case about not doing her work, had chirped at her in that middle-class teacherly voice . . . and had gotten, "Whatever . . ." in response.

I think Mandie saw something in my face at that moment of realiza-tion, too. She did attend my office hour that day. Instead of launch-ing into my usual lecture about how she needed to try harder (which assumed that she *wanted* to try harder, and for *me*), I asked her about one small detail in those two paragraphs she had written. It was an off-hand remark about not having running water in the house where she grew up, and what she told me at that moment turned into a lengthy account of growing up Black in the presence of extreme rural poverty in the Deep South, where she had lived until very recently. At the end of it, I asked her, "How did you even get here?" By that, I meant, "How did you focus enough to graduate high school? How did you get out of there? How did you develop aspirations to attend college? And where did you get the courage to move all the way to Michigan to attend a semi-urban community college?" She somehow knew what I was asking and answered these questions and more with a resolve and inner strength I had never seen from her before. Mandie was talking, a lot, to me, and she was damn smart; she was strong and determined. I might have never seen this side of her had it not been for her choice to come to my office hour that day. She had an essay, several of them, maybe a book to write. Our relationship was different after that. She passed my class, and shook my hand on her way out the door the last day. Given where we had started, this simple gesture was huge. I didn't see Mandie for a couple semesters and wondered from time to time what had happened with her. One day while waiting for an elevator in the crowded lobby of our main classroom building, I heard someone shout, "MISS REGLIN!" I turned to see Mandie about fifteen feet away. She was smiling and waving, and she was wearing nursing scrubs and an LCC nursing program nametag, which she pointed at as she held it out from her chest for me to see. I wasn't sure if she had known there was a time when I thought she didn't deserve to be in the nursing program. But somehow I think she not only knew that but knew how happy I would feel that she shared this accomplishment with me. It was a genuine, "Look what I did!" (not "in spite of you" . . . and not "because of you").

My experience with Mandie has caused me many times to wonder how many "Mandies" we assist in the writing center, students whose instructors don't see them in all of their complexities and haven't yet engaged in the kind of self-reflection Mandie caused me to do. The instructor, as an ever-present "third person" in each interaction we have with students, has more of an impact on our effectiveness than we realize. The assumptions we make about the student's relationship with their instructor are influenced by our own benevolence. When we train our staff, we teach them to redirect conversations about the instructor back toward the writing itself. Maybe we should not. Maybe part of the writing process involves processing feelings and perceptions about the person teaching them to write. What I didn't realize at the time was that I had broken through Mandie's terministic screen, a key concept in Kenneth Burke's rhetorical theory. This grid, through which we see and sift our reality, is constructed of both symbols and vocabulary and is used subconsciously by teachers and students alike to make sense of our interactions with one another. Hernandez (2015) offers a more contemporary application of this theory in *The Pedagogy of Real Talk*, explaining "we must understand [students'] terministic screen—in other words, how they view and interpret the world around them based on their gender, race, class, sexuality, and other group affiliations they may have." I was also beginning to understand the concept of intersectionality, though I didn't know what it was called at the time. It is only recently that I've learned Columbia Law School professor Kimberlé Crenshaw coined the term and uses it to describe how various pieces of our identity—including race, class, and gender—combine and contribute to the oppression of marginalized people.

The student-teacher relationship does not exist in a vacuum. It exists between people who occupy raced, classed, and gendered bodies and spaces, and it affects what and how students write and instructors respond. I am not advocating for turning students against instructors when they visit the writing center. I am advocating for listening to their stories, believing them, and not necessarily or immediately defending the instructor as we tend to do by speaking for what we're "sure they must have meant." When we encounter students who we would describe as "shy," "resistant," "defensive," or downright "angry," I am advocating for stepping back to ask ourselves where those expressions might be coming from, and when we are not sure, having the courage to say, "Tell me about what you are experiencing." As Hernandez (2015) also reminds us, "Our students are not simply students; they are people before they are students."

A close friend of many years told me that an owner of a local restaurant we both loved had been repeatedly rude to her, so much so that she was unsure whether she could eat there again or was even welcome to do so. My friend and the restauranteur settled in the U.S. after growing up in different Asian countries. "Americans have no idea how bad the tensions are between people of Asian cultures," my friend said. And she was right. I had no idea. But this time, I not only heard her talk about it but saw it firsthand when I met my friend for lunch the following week. We arrived separately, and the restaurant owner greeted me, as she had always done, with "Hi, how are you today? Good to see you! Sit anywhere you like." I waited and watched for my friend to arrive. When she did, she was greeted with a short, "Can I help you with something?" When my friend replied, "I'd like to eat lunch," she was given an eye roll and hand wave that meant either "Have a seat" or "Go away." My friend came to join me at the booth where I was sitting, and all during the meal, our interactions with the restaurant owner were different. Years ago, I would have dismissed this as simply two people—my friend and the restauranteur—who didn't like each other. I would have tried to make my friend feel better by explaining that I had seen the restaurant owner, during very busy times, exhibit some shortness and dismissiveness toward others, which was true. My own discomfort would have caused me to try to smooth things over. But my growing awareness and what I had witnessed left me knowing that what I had seen was clearly a form of racism in action. This example is important for me because it reminds me that our students don't live in writing centers, in the academic environment, or even on campus at our community college. They don't work full time or spend all day in an environment where we say that diversity is celebrated, where those who provide teaching and support services are at least somewhat aware of the importance of inclusivity and have attended workshops like Safe Zone training. They spend much of their time in the world outside of academia where there isn't even a pretense of such values.

On a recent trip to Los Angeles, my husband and I visited a souvenir shop. We were the only ones in the store, and as we walked around talking and laughing, picking up small objects, trying on hats and taking photos, the middle-aged Asian man who presumably owned the store sat behind the counter with his head down, reading a book. However, the moment a young, Black man entered through the front doors, the shop owner jumped off his stool and stood watching his every move. The young man walked around the store, looking but not touching anything. I'll bet he knew better. After a few minutes, he approached the counter to ask if the store was hiring. In his preliminary browsing, he was perhaps trying to show an interest in the products on display, or just getting a feel for the place, maybe working up the courage to ask for a job. The response he received was quick and dismissive, and he left immediately. Years ago, I would not have noticed this interaction between the shop owner and the young man, nor would I have been able to examine it the way I did. Now my semi-wokeness allows me to reflect and make connections. The marginalized students who visit our classrooms and writing centers lead lives that are dominated by daily interactions like these. Being profiled this way is the default experience for them.

And though we think of academic spaces, and certainly our writing centers, as places where people value the lived experiences of all and celebrate the great diversity that surrounds us, the "we" in this line of thinking is often white, middle-class people like me who see this environment through the lenses of benevolence and privilege. And thus, a type of oppression is perpetuated. This is not simply a "problem" to "solve," and it is not the domain of one race or another. It is complex and multi-layered, and it requires self-reflection against the experiences of other people. Many education reformers, including Bruffee (2002), argue in favor of seeking common ground and focusing on cultivating similarities with marginalized students. But the luxury to focus on similarities rather than difference has become problematic for me, as it, too, seems rooted in white privilege. For marginalized students, the elements of their identity that earned them the label of "marginalized" are ever-present. They have historically had to "struggle for voice and recognition in ways that highlight identity," again as hooks (2015) explains, drawing on the experience of constructing identity as a writer: "If long-standing structures of hierarchy and domination were not still in place and daily reinscribed, calling attention to a writer's race, gender, class or sexual practice would illuminate work, expand awareness and understanding."

For me, for now, my focus is both inward and outward, centered on my own developing awareness, continuing to nurture it within myself and helping to cultivate it in others—those I work with, those I train as writing assistants, colleagues who encounter "problem students" and don't understand what else they can do when they've tried "everything" already. It's about rhetorical listening, defined by Ratcliffe (2006) as an "openness that a person may choose to assume in relation to any person, text or culture" (17). The key word in this definition for me is *choose*. Interrogating my own privilege has caused me to see that I have the choice to hear and believe the stories of marginalized colleagues and students, and I also have the choice to question and even ignore stories of difference when they disrupt my own comfort level. Rhetorical listening involves decisive, deliberate, intentional truth-seeking in experiences related by other people, regardless of how those experiences reflect upon the raced and classed space I occupy. I'm finding myself focused a lot more intently on the faces of students I perceive to be marginalized when they come in to the writing center to ask for help. I'm finding myself listening for what is not being said when a student tells me their instructor dislikes them. Listening to and believing the narratives of individual people helps me gain some understanding about what I cannot see or experience firsthand. It reveals truths about what it means to be Black in a space that has been historically white. Watching how those who are non-white, who are non–middle class, who are non-native English speakers engage with that space tells me we have a lot of work yet to do—even the well-intentioned among us. If students are not permitted to interact with the world the same way I can, how does this change the way they engage with the classroom or writing center environment? If I cannot acknowledge that I see the world as a white, middle-class, mid-career, female faculty member, to whom a lot remains invisible, how can I engage effectively with both the staff and students whom I teach and serve in the writing center?

The conversations I am now willing and able to have—with my own students, with students who visit the writing center and with staff who work there—have shifted. I am aware that how we look at students and what we see absolutely affects the pedagogical decisions we make, however subconsciously. Lindquist (2004) advocates practicing strategic empathy: "Just as Ratcliffe argues for the importance of strategic listening to learn how to intervene in the meaning-making processes of others, I suggest that teachers can listen to students to know not only how, but who to be with them. They can strategically perform the role of learners, just as, perhaps, the ethnographer puts on an attitude of naiveté." Lindquist (2004) goes on to criticize the field of composition pedagogy (and I would say, by extension, writing center pedagogy):

> If the field has been quick to recognize that writing instruction is a political process, it has been slower in attending to the complexity, particularity, and situatedness of this process. There is growing concern, as the scholarship on these pedagogies matures (see, for example, David Seitz's review essay "Hard lessons"), that even strategies designed to make students aware of their class positions have not always worked from a deep understanding of what is at stake for students in accepting new ways of interpreting their lives.

I am in a vulnerable early stage of awareness about how my whiteness affects my relationships with the students in my classroom and those who visit and work in our writing center. But I cannot allow my own desire for self-protection to cause me to recoil from conversations like those this book will promote.

I used to be one of those white women who said she was "colorblind," who said she "didn't *see* color" and who was self-absorbed in the personal satisfaction she gained from working with such a diverse population of students, focusing on what they had in common and how well everybody got along when simply given an opportunity to do so. I was—I am, still—guilty of benevolence in all of its many forms. The difference is that I have begun to see it now, and I cannot simply ignore or accept it the same way anymore. O'Brien (2001) complicates the notion of "colorblindness" after interviewing thirty anti-racists and studying the rhetoric they use to describe their various journeys. After confronting many examples of a rhetoric of colorblindness in interviews, O'Brien

(2001) observes "that these individuals are not simply 'not colorblind'—they both are and are not, depending on who's looking and how they are looking" (p. 55). O'Brien (2001) ultimately concludes that color-blindness is multidimensional and explores the "implications of the existence of multiple antiracisms" (p. 60) yet clearly recognizes it "as a way for the majority of white Americans to pretend like there is no more racism and to justify their lack of support for any further policy solutions for race-related problems" (p. 45). O'Brien's (2001) analysis here draws on Frankenberg's earlier study, in which thirty white women were interviewed, choosing, instead of "colorblindness," the phrase "'race and power evasiveness' . . . because it is used to avoid confronting the existence of racial inequality and the power differentials inherent in such inequality" (as cited in O'Brien, 2001, p. 45). Frankenberg (1993) goes on to explain that ". . . rather than complete nonacknowledgment of any kind of difference, power evasion involves a selective attention to difference, allowing into conscious scrutiny—even conscious embrace—of those differences that make the speaker feel good but continuing to evade by means of partial description, euphemism, and self-contradiction those that make the speaker feel bad" (pp. 156–157).

I have begun to actively seek out my colleagues of color, share what I think I've observed with them and lean on them to tell me where my thinking might be misguided. At a professional conference, I sat next to two Black colleagues during a session where a brief but inappropriate vignette exhibiting cultural appropriation was shared. I looked around the room and noticed the white people laughing, while the People of Color remained stoic. Discussing the session with my two colleagues later, I said, "It bothered me, too, and I'm not even sure why." "Oh, but you do know why," one of them said. She was right. The vignette—meant to be humorous—was horribly racist. My administrative supervisor approached me midway through the current semester to ask if a student could switch sections and join my class. When she told me who his current instructor was, a young, Black faculty member, and explained that they'd not been able to get along, I asked without much thought, "There isn't some racist bullshit going on here, is there?" The ease with which I asked this question surprised me, as it would not have occurred to me to even think of such a thing twenty years ago. When encountering the phrase "colored people" in a white student's essay this semester, I not only cringed and marked it, scrolling, "people of color" in the margin, I also added, "This term is racist and offensive. Let's talk about it." O'Brien (2001) refers to "a larger variety of socially acceptable responses" that whites can employ compared with People of Color "without as much risk of stigma" (pp. 79–80). Of this I am aware. Yet the fact that I find myself saying out loud what I am seeing about race is an important step in coming to terms with my own developing awareness.

One of the most important things I implore my white colleagues to do is shut up and listen and learn to pay attention to the things our colleagues of color share. One of Bonilla-Silva's (2018) recommendations for personal change among whites seeking to confront their own color-blindness is to "read as much as you can on anti-racism" (p. 243). The reading I have engaged in as I write this chapter represents my own first attempt to absorb the scholarship of a discipline far outside my own area of expertise. Those who have entered the conversation in critical race pedagogy long ago will no doubt recognize my newness to it. I feel like one of my own writing students who is passionate about an idea, does some research and reading, and then struggles to synthesize that which she has learned with her own experience and reasoning because she is not yet educated enough to fully enter the conversation. At the same time, I feel like one of those students who visits the writing center, states that their paper is a mess, presents it to someone more experienced and is then told, "You're on the right track, and you seem to understand this better than you think you do." And this kind of feedback from trusted People of Color who are colleagues and friends gives me the courage to start making my own discoveries and to trust that I'm seeing what I think I see. I'm trying to follow Bonilla-Silva's (2018) advice to "keep constant external checks" as I try to stay "on the right path" (p. 245).

O'Brien's (2001) definition of anti-racists is people who "have committed themselves, in thought, action and practice, to dismantling racism" (p. 4). Early on in my long path to semi-woke, I might have casually described myself as "antiracist," meaning, as many white people do when we use this term, simply "against racism." Who, after all, wouldn't want to be "antiracist"? But now I see the color-blind racist ideology embedded in how whites use such terms. I am humbled by the recognition that I have a long way to go before I could ever claim to be an anti-racist, much less an ally. Labeling oneself with terms like these requires firm conviction and awesome responsibility. Martinez's 2018 keynote at the National Conference on Peer Tutoring in Writing, titled "The responsibility of privilege: A critical race conversation for allies and accomplices," urged those of us in attendance to consider the "very real danger, risk, and consequences associated with true allyship" (p. 231). "If you are witness to a person in hijab being beaten and attacked, are you ready and willing," Martinez (2018) asks, "to jump into this attack and protect this person with your own body?" I do not possess the courage to accept these risks. But I have learned that being an accomplice means adopting a willingness to ask my white friends and colleagues to examine their own thinking about the racial spaces we occupy, in other words to "get [my] people," as Martinez (2018) put it. I offer my own narrative as a way to, in Frankenberg's (1993) words, "begin the process of 'defamiliarizing' that which is taken for granted in the white experience and . . . making visible and analyzing racial structuring of white experience." (p. 44) My thinking, action and practice are shifting. But I'm not there yet. And so, the journey before me remains long.

REFERENCES

Bonilla-Silva, E. (2018). *Racism without Racists: Color-blind Racism and the Persistence of Racial Inequality in America* (5th ed.). Lanham, MD: Rowman & Littlefield.

Bruffee, K. A. (2002). Taking the common ground. *Change, 34*(1), 10–17. doi:10.1080/000 91380209601830.

Frankenberg, R. (1993). *White Women, Race Matters: The Social Construction of Whiteness.* Minneapolis, MN: University of Minnesota Press.

Hernandez, P. (2015). *The Pedagogy of Real Talk: Engaging, Teaching and Connecting with Students at Risk.* Thousand Oaks, CA: Corwin.

hooks, b. (2000). Learning in the shadow of race and class. *The Chronicle of Higher Education, 47*(12), B14–16. Retrieved from https://www.chronicle.com/article/Learning-in-the-Shadow-of-Race/6422.

hooks, b. (2015). Writing without labels. *Appalachian Heritage, 43*(4), 9+. Retrieved from http://appalachianheritage.net.

Lindquist, J. (2004). Class affects, classroom affectations: Working through the paradoxes of strategic empathy. *College English, 67*(2), 187–209. Retrieved from http://www2.ncte.org/resources/journals/college-english/.

Martinez, A. Y. (2018). The Responsibility of Privilege: A Critical Race Counterstory Conversation. *Peitho, 21*(1), 212–233. Retrieved from http://peitho.cwshrc.org/the-responsibility-of-privilege-a-critical-race-counterstory-conversation/.

O'Brien. E. (2001). *Whites Confront Racism: Antiracists and their Paths to Action.* Lanham, MD: Rowman & Littlefield.

Ratcliffe, K. (2006). *Rhetorical Listening: Identification, Gender, Whiteness.* Carbondale, IL: Southern Illinois University Press.

10

STORIES OF ACTIVIST ALLIES IN THE WRITING CENTER

Dianna Baldwin and Trixie G. Smith

We begin with our stories. To situate ourselves—our experiences, values, commitments. To say these are the roots we draw from, as well as the injustices we fight against. To show how and why we came to our own understandings of allyship and activist work. And to situate ourselves in a complicated place and time amidst national movements such as #MeToo, #IbelieveHer, and #BlackLivesMatter, but also amidst very local, institutional concerns about the safety of our colleagues and students, young women (in sports) in particular. And to emphasize that stories matter and, as Chimamanda Ngozi Adichie tells us in her TED talk, there is a danger in listening to just one story.

DIANNA'S STORY

Born in the coal mining mountains of West Virginia, my parents abandoned the coal miner's life and moved the family to the Blue Ridge Mountains of Virginia in the Appalachian range—pronounced *app-a-latch-an*—when I was two years old. Rather than a coal miner's daughter, I am a hillbilly. The town I grew up in had *no* diversity that I saw. There were no African American kids in our schools, no Latinos, no Asians. Our little town and surrounding areas in the mountains were about as homogenized as you could get. The only time I ever witnessed any diversity was when we would drop out of the mountains into North Carolina to visit family, and that wasn't often.

But I knew I needed more than that lifestyle to sustain me. I wanted adventure, an education, and a way of life that wasn't in a factory eight hours a day, my lungs filling with toxins. So, at the age of 18, I left home, and real forms of diversity began to enter into my existence. It didn't all happen at once, as that would have been overwhelming, and I would have turned tail and run back to the mountains. But with

https://doi.org/10.7330/9781646421534.c010

each move, I found new people, new cultures, and new ways of thinking and being.

However, that growth also brought pain and embarrassment. While still a member of the white dominant culture, no longer did my form of speaking fit in with the majority. It was in the West that I truly experienced a feeling of alienation. I was referred to as John Boy: not because I had discovered my lesbianess or queerness, but because my speech most closely resembled what these folks had heard on the popular television show *The Waltons*. It didn't help that my last name is Baldwin (you can look it up). My speech was made fun of by my "friends," and I often had to find a different way of saying something to get them to understand. The pain of these experiences left me not wanting to speak for fear of sounding "stupid."

After years of travel and living all over the states, though, I returned home after the passing of my grandfather to deal with his belongings. During a huge yard sale (not estate, just plain ole yard), I met many of my grandfather's friends, but what stuck with me was the conversation I had with one little lady. After confessing that I'd been raised a stone's throw from the spot where we were standing, she remarked "you don't sound like yer from 'round here." I was no longer hillbilly enough to fit in here, but not Standard American English enough to fit in other places. Being alienated in the big world was one thing, but feeling alienated in my mountains . . . words can't express.

The forty years since I left those mountains have been filled with adventure and heartache. My eight years in the Navy taught me the importance of "Don't ask, don't tell." So much so, that when I ventured to grad school in the South as a 40-something adult, I adhered to that rule, telling no one of my personal life. So, my first experiences in a writing center weren't any different than any other job. I worked, kept to myself for the most part, and went home to my partner every night. Trust was not something that came easy.

After six years of grad school, I joined the ranks of academia as the associate director of a Big Ten writing center. It was at this point that I decided I would not live closeted anymore. I learned growing up that I had the right to live my life as I chose as long as it did not interfere with the rights of others. And I believe in that right for *everyone*. I have white privilege, and I'm painfully, at times, aware of that. But what that privilege can afford me is the opportunity to offer others with less privilege, those who are, at times, more marginalized than me, an ally.

TRIXIE'S STORY

I grew up in the Deep South where I went to church for one thing or another 4–5 times a week, sometimes more when I was older. I attended school at this same Southern Baptist church, which was mostly white but with a range of class positions, until fourth grade. I then moved to the public system that was still under court order to desegregate. I heard teachers complain about "those problem kids" who were being bused in, away from their own African American neighborhoods and friends. Even I, a naive fourth-grader, could understand that this busing "solution" was actually a problem creating anger, frustration, and kids who resented spending so much of their day on a school bus, bypassing the school in their neighborhood to help equalize numbers in some other school.

A dozen years later, as a teacher in this same system, I experienced even more of these bad solutions to inequality in the schools. I taught a year of middle school with a student population that identified solely as African American, which made sense for its neighborhood location (segregated neighborhoods are a whole other issue not to be addressed here), but this school was becoming a magnet school the next year—the middle school devoted to the creative and performing arts—in order to draw in other students (read: white students). We spent the whole year suffering through sand-blasting, hammering, and the closing of resources in order to prepare this school for its new inhabitants. Again, I understood the anger and frustration of the students. In fact, I felt my own, but wasn't really sure what to do about it at that point.

These frustrations took me back to the first writing center I ever encountered at my undergraduate liberal arts college. I was one of the first two peer tutors at this new center, the opening of which coincided with the launch of the new sports program and the recruitment of international students and People of Color who had never been intentionally recruited before at this predominantly white institution. I couldn't help but draw connections between these two events and wonder about the true goals of the writing center at this institution.

A few more years down the road, I left teaching public school in order to attend graduate school—still in the South, but on the eastern coast rather than the gulf. During this transformational time, I came out to first myself, then others, about my lesbian identity, I pursued women's and queer studies as well as the field of composition and rhetoric, and learned much about growing ideas of intersectionality as well as systemic racism, classism, sexism, and homophobia—both in texts and in lived experience. During this time, I worked in several different writing centers at the university and at local community colleges. I worked to weave together all of these various interests, imperatives, and desires for a more diverse, egalitarian academy, and if not that, then the microcosm of the writing center.

It is this original sense of helplessness and unfairness, coupled with the reality of power as the white director of a large writing center, that has come to drive my need for and philosophies of allyship.

DEFINITIONS

Defining and understanding allyship can be tricky business. We all know what an ally is, right? It's the person who's got your back, the person who stands beside you regardless of what happens. In fact, when things are at their worst, an ally doesn't run away or pretend you no longer exist.

But the position of allies when we are discussing identity and positionality, e.g., race, gender, ability, or sexuality, is often hotly debated and a bit complicated. As Neisha-Anne S. Green (2016) advises "in our efforts to help [or be allies], we need to be aware of creating new issues or making old ones worse" (Not Your Average [Insert Stereotype Here] section, para. 1). Similar advice comes from Anne Harris and Stacey Holman Jones (2017) when they discuss the need for allies to avoid believing they feel the same way or have similar experiences to those they are trying to support (p. 566). Kimberlé Crenshaw (1991) explains that "[w]hile gender, race, and class intersect to create the particular context in which women of color experience violence, certain choices made by 'allies' can reproduce intersectional subordination within the very resistance strategies designed to respond to the problem" (p. 1262). After witnessing this type of allyship, we begin to doubt that anyone who doesn't experience our same marginalization or share our particular identity can truly help our cause.

But being an ally is also an identity, and it can be fluid and ever changing. It also intersects with all of our other identities and positions. This intersectionality means that we practice allyship from different places of being. The practice of allyship grows as we grow and as needs or circumstances change. Consequently, there is no definitive way of being an ally. Just as Victor Del Hierro, Daisy Levy, and Margaret Price (2016) note, there are no checklists for how to be a good ally; there are only experiences and stories (p. 20). In fact, they conclude that being an ally is an orientation, it is a way of approaching the world and the people around us. We call this being an activist ally because an allied orientation should always lead to action (or perhaps being an accomplice, as Greene [2016] would say).

We both try to promote and practice activist allyship in our day-to-day lives; it is our orientation, so it only makes sense that this comes through in our work in the writing center. In fact, we like to think of the center as an allied space. However, it is not without pain, without tension or mistakes, as our center has gone through regular growing pains over the past ten years as we've strived to think about what an allied space is or does and then create it. Crenshaw (1991) warns that the elision of multiple identities and positions can result in the subordination or oppression of others even when trying to support them (p. 1242). With Crenshaw in mind, Lorena Garcia (2016) argues that we need to be constantly "challenging our students as well as ourselves to think and dialogue about the interconnections of various social locations and to practice the application of intersectionality in our analyses" (pp. 103–4). While Garcia is discussing a classroom environment here, it certainly applies to writing center environments. It is only through this constant dialoguing and critical thinking that we can work through the tensions and continue to practice activist allyship in the center.

CREATING SPACE

Not surprisingly, you can't just declare a space allied or open or safe enough or brave[1] and expect everyone to believe you and to just "come on in." You have to practice this openness and allyship in meaningful and visible ways; you have to create a space that is safe/brave enough for risk taking to seem feasible. We have tried (and are always trying) to do this in a variety of ways. We begin by asking our consultants to make the space *their* own, not some universal (read white, heterosexual, middle class) version of home.[2]

Walking into our center, your eyes are drawn to two things: individualized ceiling tiles and the matrix of colors (26 different colors to be exact) across the far wall. Our consultants designed/painted this matrix after debating the uses of color in the center and how color affects both them and our clients. The ceiling tiles have been collected over the years as we ask each consultant to create a tile that represents them in some way: their interests, their personalities, their homes. The range of art and sayings across the tiles sends a concrete message of diversity and inclusion.

---

1. For an excellent collection of articles about "Writing centers as brave/r spaces," see Martini (2017).

2. For discussions of home as metaphor for the writing center, see McKinney (2013); Grimm (1999).

Toys throughout the center are another tool for making the space welcoming and suitable for risk taking. We've had students and faculty alike tell us how much they enjoy the idea of playing with Play-Doh, creating figures from pipe cleaners, and just manipulating various Tangles and squishy toys while talking about their writing or assignments. They have attributed stress release, creativity, the ability to concentrate, and simple enjoyment to the various toys. We're beginning to see toys scattered across offices and meeting spaces all over campus as those who have been to the center take this practice back with them. But we've also learned from some of our consultants that too many things can be off-putting to students of color who have experienced false accusations of theft or have been followed around a store to make sure they don't steal anything.

We have also worked to convey messages of allyship with our formal materials. As many centers have done, we added places in both our intake forms and our appointment forms for clients to note their preferred pronouns, if they so choose. We provide consultant bios in our appointment system to help clients make informed decisions about their appointments, choosing consultants who will meet their various personal/professional/disciplinary/religious/cultural needs. More recently, we've been working on statements about Students Rights to their Own Language, pronoun options and usage, and trigger warnings for consultants.[3]

Being open to a wide range of writing/composing needs is also an important tool for encouraging diversity in thought and practice and developing an ally orientation. For many years, The Writing Center @ MSU has been known in name and practice as a space for multimedia work.[4] Student remix projects decorate the center, from cross-stitch plaques representing tutoring philosophies to dioramas of the center, jukeboxes, and paper dolls that represent the various roles of the center and its consultants. Various languages and images are also featured throughout the center.

But you need more than things to make people feel welcome. You need people who are welcoming and diverse. If potential clients can see someone like them in the writing center, they are more likely to come

---

3. These are all complicated issues that warrant their own time and space for examining pros and cons and consequences for both clients and consultants. But for here, we want to acknowledge that these efforts are all tied to the work of making our center accessible, writing-centered, student-centered, and social justice oriented.

4. See Sheridan, D. & Inman, J. (Eds.). (2010). *Multiliteracy Centers: Writing Center Work, New Media, and Multi-modal Rhetoric*. New York: Hampton Press, Inc.

to the center and return. The same goes for future consultants. In 1991 Gail Y. Okawa suggested that the way to build truly collaborative relationships across writers and tutors was to first actively recruit and hire tutors "to mirror the cultural, linguistic, gender, and class diversity of our students" and then to train them to see writing consultations as mired in cultural expectations and experiences (pp. 14–15). Twenty years later, Harry Denny (2010) challenged us to consider who is "us" and who is "them" in any particular writing center context as he questioned the "dissonance between writing center personnel and the people with whom they worked" (p. 5). Denny suggests one solution for this disconnect is "facing" the center, knowing the multitude of "whos" present in our centers, "both marginal and privileged," while also considering the politics of this facing—"how we *face* and to what impact" (p. 6). It is this kind of thinking that has influenced our ongoing recruitment efforts.

RECRUITMENT PRACTICES

Our consultants are always our strongest resource, so when we wanted to think purposefully and strategically about ways to make our center staff more diverse, we talked to our staff. One of our conversations was about intentionally diverse recruiting as mentioned above. As administrators we began sending our recruitment letters to faculty and staff who had more contact with diverse students and were thus more likely to recommend diverse students. This included the director of the LBGT Resource Center and faculty representatives with student organizations focused around activism and identity. We also targeted instructors teaching classes in programs such as Gender Studies, Chicano Studies, African and African-American Studies, American Indian and Indigenous Studies, and others. We also reached out to our own personal networks of diverse instructors and colleagues.[5] We wouldn't say this approach reached our expectations at first, but it is continuing to grow and expand, so we will continue down this path.

For their part, consultants also used their personal networks to recruit and help retain diverse students (more on this later). One graduate student who identified as Chicanx, for example, recruited three other Latinx students from three different programs. They in turn have recruited other graduate students; many of them also teach

5. Numerous stories and studies have noted that faculty of color, queer faculty, and other minority faculty often serve as unofficial mentors and advisors for students who also identify as other in some way. This is often unpaid and even unacknowledged labor. See Turner, González, & Wood (2008); Matthew (2016, Nov. 23).

undergraduate courses and have also begun nominating undergraduates for our Writing Center Theory and Practice course. The tension here, not surprisingly, is that students make decisions about how to use their personal networks based on a range of factors and their own experiences in the center. So, yes, this helpful Chicanx student has recruited a number of students of color. However, an African American consultant who is more skeptical of the openness of the center has not been as apt to recruit other African Americans even though her own research says that de-racializing the space means recruiting more diverse consultants.

We also value diversity in terms of major and discipline. While our center is housed in the College of Arts and Letters, we serve the whole university, so we recruit and hire across the university. Having students from the sciences and social sciences, as well as the humanities, ensures a variety of perspectives and fosters productive dialogue about center policy and practice. We have also been open to hiring across and supporting students with varying ableness, hires that often remind us of the different needs for accommodation that our clients can also bring to the center. Hiring from such varied locations, however, also means that students come with a range of career and curricular goals and thus different commitments to the "job" and the "work" of the center.

RETENTION PRACTICES

Once we've recruited our staff, we strive to keep our retention rate high. We want people to enjoy coming to work most days, and we try to create an environment that promotes both a feeling of satisfaction and a brave enough space in which to work and even thrive. The space itself is described above, but in what other ways can we promote a safe/satisfying work space for all of our consultants?

First, we acknowledge that people are different. We don't even differentiate undergraduate vs. graduate consultants except when mandated by law (e.g., only graduate students can approve timesheets). Instead, we embrace difference and support our consultants in meaningful ways we hope will help them grow as consultants, writers, and allies.

One of these efforts includes a flattened hierarchy in the center. Rather than just the administrative staff making the decisions that steer the center, a flattened hierarchy offers those interested in the process a voice. Students can participate in a range of committees and programs which allow them to share their expertise and/or develop new skills. Similarly, a focus on continued professional development provides space for relationship building, learning, and sharing expertise. For example, like many, we conduct regular staff meetings on a variety of student-requested topics, university programs and resources, and writing center theory and practice. These practices not only help retain our staff, but also strengthen intersectionality, diversity, and active allyship.

We have also used research as a way to build community while also effecting change in the center. For example, groups of administrators and consultants have conducted research on the idea of community in our center, the needs of multilingual writers in sessions, the factors that racialize a space like the center, and other topics of diversity and outreach. They have also developed workshops and written blog posts on topics like microaggressions, Students Rights to their Own Language, and working with diverse learning styles. In addition, we are fortunate enough, through special grant funding as well as partnership funding, to be able to support this research financially and to be able to take our consultants to our state, regional, and (inter)national conferences where they can share their research and build both their personal and center networks. Not surprisingly, this retention practice can also serve as a recruitment practice, particularly at the graduate level.

Mentoring is a top priority in our writing center and is crucial for retention. This happens in two ways: organic and organized. Organized mentoring takes on many forms. Often staff come to us and ask for our assistance and a formal mentorship plan is put in place. This can be for help with a thesis or dissertation, with job preparation, or some other project. But we also have a mentoring coordinator. This person is tasked with setting up mentoring partnerships. The coordinator will ask some-one who has been in the center for a while if they would like to mentor a new consultant. It is important to note that this form of mentoring is also an attempt to create allyship. As Del Hierro, Levy, and Price note (2016), "allyship is not a state to be achieved, but a community-based process of making" (p. 2).

This type of allyship is best achieved, however, through organic men-toring. Organic mentoring, as the name implies, happens naturally and without any prompting. This type of relationship often creates strong bonds for those involved and remains intact far beyond what most organized mentoring connections do. What does organic mentoring look like? It looks like service on a center committee that results in teamwork on a very specific project or program. It looks like two people chatting during a lull in consultations and soon realizing they have a research interest in common. From that conversation comes a center-related project with other consultants involved, and suddenly you have a "community-based process of making" where those involved negotiate issues of power and difference, among other things, to bring their project to fruition.

Both organic and organizational mentoring are crucial for our writing center. This multipronged approach ensures that everyone has the opportunity to learn and grow from those around them and perhaps experience a sense of allyship among their peers.

WHAT TENSIONS EXIST IN THIS STANCE AND ENACTMENT?

The work of creating a diverse population of consultants also comes with a variety of needs and tensions: tensions between consultants, consultants and administration, consultants and clients, and even internal tensions when there are conflicting goals and beliefs, or students feel pulled in different directions by differing programs and responsibilities. There are times when being an ally to one is perceived as being disloyal to another.

Something as necessary as being mentors (allies) can create tension. One example of this is a study we attempted to conduct with graduate coordinators one semester. Being a graduate assistant/coordinator for such a big center is a time-consuming, difficult job. We thought we could help coordinators understand a little about how they work by conducting a time management study. From the beginning, we told all coordinators that this was NOT intended to police their time, but to help them better understand their own work practices and to help us make sure we were allowing enough time for the duties assigned. We reiterated that we understood some jobs fluctuated timewise over the course of the semester. Some coordinators understood we were trying to mentor them while others immediately felt policed, micromanaged, and/or scrutinized. Some even reported being made to feel guilty about how they used their personal time when they saw it in print. Complaints about our "nefarious" intentions definitely created tension and distrust across our relationships. But eventually it also allowed us to have conversations about these feelings and why they existed for some. Part of this difference was tied to previous working relationships, experiences with school, and cultural beliefs about authority figures. Even though the data we hoped to collect never came to fruition, we feel it was a successful mentorship opportunity in the end because of the very open conversations that came out of this endeavor.

Bringing together so many different people in the limited space/ place of the writing center is bound to create conflict and tension. But we don't view this as a bad thing. Part of being an activist ally is learning through and acting through (despite?) these differences. These tensions encourage us to continue to develop and support the diversity of our center. It is only through different cultural values, work ethics, religious and political positions that we can learn from one another and continue to grow as individuals and as a center. This is certainly how we have continued to grow as administrators who desire to be activist allies in the center and in our own personal lives.

DIANNA'S AND TRIXIE'S STORIES: CONTINUED

As we sit in Grand Traverse Pie Company finishing this piece, we are reminded of the changes that face both of us in this ongoing story. Dianna prepares to leave MSU and take on the directorship of her own, albeit small, writing center in rural Virginia. She knows she will take her commitment to allyship with her, but wonders how it might need to change and morph to fit this new environment and people. Trixie considers how to ensure she hires a new associate director with shared commitments to diversity and allyship, and wonders how Dianna's departure will affect the community we have built over the past ten years. Collectively, we know that one of the reasons activist allyship is an orientation is because it must continually adapt to the changing people and circumstances both locally and globally. We offer these actions and orientations from our center as descriptive, to share possibilities, not as prescriptive or as a strict model to follow. Through our storytelling, we challenge others to join us as we actively use our individual writing centers, as well as the field itself, to enact change in the academy and in the broader community.

REFERENCES

Adichie, C. N. (2009). The danger of a single story. Retrieved from www.ted.com.
Crenshaw, K. (1991). Mapping the margins: Intersectionality, identity politics, and violence against women of color. *Stanford Law Review, 43*(6), 1241–99.
Del Hierro, V., Levy, D. & Price, M. (2016). We are here: Negotiating difference and alliance in spaces of cultural rhetorics. *Enculturation: A Journal of Rhetoric, Writing, and Culture*. Retrieved from http://enculturation.net/we-are-here.
Denny, H. (2010). *Facing the Center: Toward an Identity Politics of One-to-One Mentoring*. Logan: Utah State University Press.
Garcia, L. (2016). Intersectionality. *Kalfou, 3*(1), 102–06. Utah University Press.
Green, N. S. (2016). The re-education of Neisha-Anne S. Green: A close look at the damaging effects of "a standard approach," the benefits of code-meshing, and the role allies play in this work. *Praxis: A Writing Center Journal, 14*(1). Retrieved from http://www.praxisuwc.com/green-141.
Grimm, N. M. (1999). *Good Intentions: Writing Center Work for Post Modern Times*. Portsmouth: Heinemann.

Grutsch McKinney, J. (2013). *Peripheral Visions for Writing Centers*. Logan: Utah State University Press.

Harris, A., & Jones, S. H. (2017). Feeling fear, feeling queer: The peril and potential of queer terror. *Qualitative Inquiry, 23*(7), 561–68.

Martini, R. H. & Webster, T. (Eds.). (2017). Writing centers as brave/r spaces. *Special Issue of The Peer Review, 1*(2). Retrieved from http://thepeerreview-iwca.org/issues/braver-spaces/.

Matthew, P. A. (2016, Nov. 23). What is faculty diversity worth to a university? *The Atlantic*. Retrieved from https://www.theatlantic.com/.

Okawa, G.Y., Fox, T., Chang, L. J. Y., Windson, S. R., Chavez Jr., F. B., & Hayes, L. (1991). Multi-cultural voices: Peer tutoring and critical reflection in the writing center. *WCJ, 12*(1), 11–33.

Sheridan, D. & Inman, J. (Eds.). (2010). *Multiliteracy Centers: Writing Center Work, New Media, and Multi-modal Rhetoric*. New York: Hampton Press, Inc.

Turner, C. S. V., González, J. C., Wood, J. L. (2008). Faculty of color in academe: What 20 years of literature tells us. *Journal of Diversity in Higher Education, 1*(3), 139–168.

AFTERWORD

Neisha-Anne S. Green and Frankie Condon

As many of the contributors to this volume have pointed out, writing center studies has persisted in claiming and celebrating performances of care, comfort, and empathy, even as those performances have been called out by scholars of colour as failures and exposed as mere theatre. Collectively, we argue in this book that intersectionality is an oppositional praxis aimed at the nexus of system, structure, and institutional powers that sustain and reproduce inequality and injustice for women of colour, LGBTQ+ peoples, for poor and working-class peoples, for disabled peoples, and, particularly, for those who make their lives at the intersections and overlaps among and between these identities. Intersectionality creates the conditions in which prophetic love—the affiliative relation of alliance, camaraderie, accompliceship—aligns, strengthens, and gives heft to our collective struggles for equality, justice, freedom, and their offspring: opportunity, access, and economic, social, and political uplift. Without hard work—without lived struggle in which we walk the talk, however, this position is mere possibility, mere idealism.

The nature of this hard work, we must confess, seems self-evident to us. Or, perhaps, more accurately, we are convinced that both the necessity for this work and its nature have already been explained, repeatedly.

Although Stephen North's *The Idea of a Writing Center* is perhaps the most cited piece of writing center scholarship in our field's history, in 1994 North published a follow-up essay in which he analyzed, critiqued, and revised the claims of that most famous work. Readers will recall the original essay as the source of that truly exhausted adage, "We make better writers, not better writing," and in which he argued that rather than being peripheral to writing programs, writing centers should be the institutional center and locus for the teaching of writing (Barrett et al., 2008, p. 69). In *Revisiting the Idea of a Writing Center*, North addresses the failure of writing centers, generally, to change institutional commitments to traditional writing instruction. Rather than becoming or

https://doi.org/10.7330/9781646421534.c011

acting as "the locus of any larger consciousness" about either the political dimensions of writing pedagogy or best practices in the teaching of
writing, North writes,

> there is a very strong tendency for [the writing center] to become the
> place whose existence serves simultaneously to locate a wrongness (in
> this case, illiteracy, variously conceived) *in* a set of persons (and in that
> sense to constitute language differences *as* a wrongness); to absolve the
> institution from further consideration of such persons, in that they have
> now been named ('basic,' remedial,' 'developmental') and 'taken care
> of'; and, not incidentally, to thereby insulate the institution from any dan-
> ger to its own configuration the differences such persons are now said to
> embody might otherwise pose. In short—and to put it in the most sinister
> terms—this particular romanticization of the writing center's institutional
> potential may actually mask its complicity in what Elspeth Stuckey has
> called the violence of literacy. (1994, p. 15)

While North does not specifically name students of colour or women
of colour, in particular, first-generation college students, students from
poor and working-class families, or LGBTQ+ students, we believe it is
reasonable to infer that those were the kinds of students he was referring
to. And just to reiterate, North raises at least the possibility of the writing
center's implication in not merely a single institution's ideological, and
thus pedagogical, violence, but also in the structural violence of higher
education writ large with particular regard to the idea of literacy, to linguistic supremacy, and to writing pedagogies in whatever site they may
be practiced—in 1994.

In 2003, Rebecca Moore Howard delivered the keynote address at the
International Writing Centers Association in Hershey, Pennsylvania, the
theme of which was "Writing Back." Speaking of postcolonial theories
of writing back (to imperialist and colonialist systems and structures
of power), Howard writes that "writing programs and writing centers
are the gatekeepers, the border police, the enforcers of standards, the
transmitters of basic skills" (2004, 5). Drawing on the work of Allistair
Pennycook, Howard notes the relationship between language, linguistic
supremacy, and the imperial enterprise: that "language is as much a site
as it is a means for struggle" (Pennycook, p. 267, as quoted in Howard
2004, p. 4). Driving her point home, Howard says

> But here's where the notion of writing back in its application to writing cen-
> ters ruptures writing back, as it is deployed in postcolonial theory, speaks
> to the experience of a colonized community after the moment of political
> independence, as it begins to forge a hybrid, syncretic language in which
> a national literature can be developed (Ashcroft, Griffiths, and Tiffin).
> We can establish no analogous position for the writing center, because the

writing center had no existence prior to an imperial moment. On the contrary, the writing center, like composition courses, is a creation of and tool of the academic endeavor to maintain linguistic and rhetorical standards; to mark writers who do not meet those standards; and to demand that they willingly accede to and adopt those standards. (2004, p. 6)

Here, Howard connects both the *idea* of a writing center and the *work* of writing centers to the imperial enterprise—not only in North America, but globally, arguing that the discourses of idealism as they are deployed in writing center studies mask the degree to which the work of writing centers is implicated in the imperial enterprise and effacing the intellectual, pedagogical, and political labour required to engage in work toward effective structural and institutional change from within the writing center. Just to reiterate, Howard's keynote was delivered in 2003 and published in the *Writing Center Journal* in 2004.

Two years after Howard's keynote address to the IWCA, Victor Villanueva delivered the keynote at the same conference in Minneapolis. Entitled "Blind: Talking about the new racism," Villanueva took up the wicked problem of racism explicitly, critiquing, in particular, the practice of "colourblindness" as a strategy for implicitly endorsing systemic, institutional, and individual racism by asserting that systems, institutions, and/or individuals do not "see" race. Speaking of the relationship between language, ideology, and worldview, Villanueva argued in his address that not only are our perspectival horizons shaped "by the language we receive and use, by trope" (2006, p. 5), "[t]hey are also shaped by the language we don't use." Villanueva asserts firmly that "[i]f we no longer speak of 'racism,' racism gets ignored" (2006, p. 5). Finally, Villanueva decries the willful ignorance of those who embrace colourblind ideology. He writes

Those of us dedicated to anti-racist pedagogy, to addressing the current state of racism find ourselves every day trying to convince folks that there really still is racism, and it's denied. In the face of all that front-page misery of hurricane Katrina, it's denied; in the face of all those brown-skinned terrorists (even when one is simply a Brazilian late for work), it's denied; even in the lack of parity in the land of opportunity, it's denied. Our rhetoric and the rhetoric of the everyday aren't jiving. We see racism. They see something else, sedimentation of a racism that was, perhaps, but not what we rail against (2006, p. 11).

Let us reiterate, Villanueva's address was delivered in 2006. And, we might add, in the years since Villanueva's IWCA keynote, between 2006 and 2018, Frankie has delivered six keynote addresses focused on race and racism, white supremacy, and linguistic supremacy to regional, national, and international writing center and writing program organizations, most recently with co-presenters Vershawn Ashanti Young (Mid-Atlantic Writing Centers Association, 2018, and Conference on Writing Across the Curriculum, 2018). In 2017, Neisha-Anne became the first woman of colour to ever deliver a keynote address at the International Writing Centers Association Conference.

One might well ask why we are still talking about racism—why are the established and emerging scholars whose work is collected in this volume *still* talking about white supremacy and its imperial linkage with linguistic supremacy? Maybe we are crazy, or maybe it's the field manifesting that form of inhumanity-as-madness characterized by endlessly repeating the same tired denials over and over and over again or, worse, offering ovations then heading home to carry on with those exercises of privilege and complicity that ensure the stability of their boats while the rest of us drown.

If we were writing this Afterword from the place to which we dream of traveling together, we'd be sitting on the porch of Neisha-Anne's house in Barbados. Neisha-Anne would be rocking in her chair, drinking a fine whiskey, and Frankie would be sitting on the step, sipping on something with rum and fruit and decorated with several paper umbrellas. Instead, Frankie writes from the University of Waterloo, in Ontario, Canada. Her University was built upon the Haldimand tract: the traditional territory of the Attawandaron (Neutral), Anishnaabeg, and Haudenosaunee peoples; land promised and given to the Six Nations, which includes six miles on each side of the Grand River. Neisha-Anne writes from American University in Washington, DC, on the traditional territory of the Nacotchtank. Further, Neisha-Anne works at a university situated on land on which enslaved peoples were forced to labour for 150 years for white families occupying that land, including the founder of the University. The land on which American University is now situated was purchased with funds accumulated, in part at least, from the proceeds of slavery (American University Working Group on the Influence of Slavery, 2019).

But why does place matter and, more particularly, why does the history of the places where we labour matter—to us? Each time Frankie hears or gives a territorial acknowledgement, she remembers the attempted genocide that was the enabling condition for the formation of her family. She feels again the profound tension between the love she and her brother have always shared and the terrible reality that her brother, Rick, who is Ojibwe, was stolen from his birth family during the era of the Federal Indian Adoption Project and placed for adoption with their white parents.[1] Neisha-Anne, whose extended family still lives in Barbados, is the descendant of slaves. She comes from a people who resisted. In fact, in 1807, when Great Britain abolished the slave trade but not slavery itself, 70,000 enslaved Barbadians rose up against white slaveholders, driving them from the plantations they had occupied, during Bussa's Rebellion. Although the Rebellion failed, it signaled the refusal of the enslaved peoples of Barbados to accept oppression as their lot and their ongoing refusal to capitulate to the institution of slavery.

Place matters. Place binds us to the condition of our becoming: to the making and fracturing of our relations, and the necessity of remaking and repairing them. Place binds us to our intertwining histories and to the necessity of telling the truth of those histories; binds us to our families and the ways in which we may have been ripped asunder by racism, by white supremacy, and by patriarchy, as well as the ways we in which we love deeply and truly, despite our separation. Place—and those relations that place both enables and signifies—makes possible embodiments and enactments of hope in which we take on those conditions that have produced our brokenness. For both of us, the writing centre is a place, both in the metonymic and the material sense, that has shaped our senses of who we are and what we do that matters as scholars, teachers, and writers—a place around which we have built our professional lives. We have seen, heard, borne witness to, and Neisha-Anne has been subjected to, racism within the writing centre. And because we don't roll as if our labour is somehow apolitical and therefore necessarily separate and distinct from our activism, writing centres have been a site for engagement: a place in which we have both felt called to speak up, to speak out, to resist racism and white supremacy.

Given the weight of our histories, the fact that we write together but still more so that we love and care for one another as chosen family is something of a miracle. Perhaps this is why Vershawn Young posited, as Wonderful Faison and Frankie wrote in their introduction to this volume, that the question of how friendships—how love and care—between People of Colour and whites can be possible is exactly the right question to be asking. But why? Why does friendship or love or care matter in a book about intersectional feminism and the work of writing centres? Martin Luther King once wrote that "Power without love is reckless and abusive, and love without power is sentimental and anemic" (King, 1967). We recognize the debt that modern anti-racism and intersectional feminism owe to those leaders of the Civil Rights movement, and,

---

1. This story is told in greater detail in Condon's 2012 monograph, *I Hope I Join the Band: Narrative, Affiliation, and Antiracist Rhetoric* (pp. 38–40).

indeed, those who struggle for justice everywhere, who have spoken so consistently and insistently of the inextricability of love from power. We follow Brittney Cooper in arguing that "[i]ntersectionality is not an account of personal identity but one of power" (2016, p. 1). And we follow Chela Sandoval in recognizing that powerful resistance—a methodology of the oppressed rooted in intersectional praxis—must draw on the wellsprings of prophetic love: that affinity and care which "undoes the 'one' that gathers the narrative, the couple, the race, into a singularity" (2000, p. 169). As Sandoval notes, "prophetic love gathers up the *mezcla*, the mixture that lives through *differential movement* between possibilities of being." This love, points out Sandoval, is the "consciousness of the 'borderlands' or '*la conciencia de la mestiza*'—not, in other words, love alone, but love that is both the location and the source of oppositional consciousness: the necessary condition for power-to" (as quoted in Condon, 2012, p. 74; Sandoval, p. 169).

INTERSECTIONALITY, POWER, AND PROPHETIC LOVE

Intersectionality is a conceptual and analytical framework conceived by Kimberlé Crenshaw as a disruption of "the tendency in social-justice movements and critical social theorizing 'to treat race and gender as mutually exclusive categories of experience and analysis'" (Cooper, 2016; Crenshaw, 1989). The emergence of intersectionality as a *thing*—a term laden with cultural cachet within progressive/Left intellectual and activist circles—has led to misunderstanding, misrepresentation, and misuse (Cooper, 2016, p. 3). We believe, with Brittney Cooper, however, that

> intersectionality's most powerful argument is . . . that institutional power arrangements, rooted as they are in relations of domination and subordination, confound and constrict the life possibilities of those who already live at the intersection of certain identity categories, even as they elevate the possibilities of those living at more legible (and privileged) points of intersection. Thus, while intersectionality should be credited with 'lifting the veil' to invoke Du Bois's metaphor of the racial 'color line,' we should remain clear that the goal of intersectionality is not to provide an epistemological mechanism to bring communities from behind the veil into full legibility. It is rather to rend the veil and make sure that no arguments are articulated to support its reconstruction. (2016, p. 9)

The in-your-face-ness of intersectional activism—its oppositionality—troubles those who continue to depend upon whitely, neoliberal notions of civility, negotiation, compromise, and patience in labours for social change. "Rending the veil" and preventing the articulation of arguments to "support its reconstruction" do not translate well into the *culture of nice* that is the habitus of the predominantly white field of writing center studies as of the predominantly white writing center. The confrontational stance that is constituted by intersectional praxis seems or, perhaps, *feels* not-nice, rude, uncaring. For us, however, the more critical question is this: to whom are we kind when we tolerate domination, subordination, marginalization, exploitation, oppression in the crucible of racism, misogyny, classism, homo- and transphobia, white supremacy, and patriarchy?

We recognize and acknowledge the deep relationship of prophetic love to power: the agency and action, to hope and meaningful change. Love, however, prophetic or not, is more easily claimed than lived and in no case, we think, is this more true than in the formation of relationships between white women and Women of Colour. Power and its historical abuse through the discourses, systems, and structures of white supremacy—historical injustice—have indelibly marked us all in ways that agitate against reciprocal, just, and caring relations. In particular, we believe that white women have learned too well to mistake submission to power for love, to imagine love as mere feeling, divorced somehow from the political—from power, its exercise, and its abuse. The historical injustices of white supremacy that have so privileged white women and crafted that privilege through the disenfranchisement and oppression of Women of Colour have perverted white women's capacity not merely to *feel* but also to *think* and to *act* powerfully in ways that are shaped by affiliative relations and the differential consciousness—the mixture—made possible by those relations. They/we have learned to expect friendship as a right and are, thus, surprised when friendship is not immediately forthcoming. We have been blind not only to the historical injustices that have made strangers of us all but also to the array of obligations and responsibilities that the legatees of systemic white supremacy and privilege bear to participate actively, fulsomely, ruthfully in challenging, resisting, opposing, and dismantling racism—without expectation of return.

In his book, *Rhetoric of Black Revolution* (1969), Arthur L. Smith argues that the Black revolutionary rhetoric exposes the hypocrisy of American democracy, and makes apparent the "festering sore," the fundamental contradiction between white America's political mythology and its quotidian sense of who should, could, does compose the body politic: "How can we divorce ourselves from the blacks and at the same time maintain our national integrity?" (p. 4). Smith calls out, in other words, the desire of white Americans to sustain both the national mythology of equality and inclusion as fundamental to American democracy and white supremacism with its separation, Otherness, and disenfranchisement of American

Peoples of Colour. We believe there is an analogic relationship between the historical discourses of predominantly white writing centres (and the predominantly white field of writing centre studies) and those of the racial state that Smith accuses of hypocrisy. The Big-D and Small-D discourses, as James Gee might say, are syncretic in the same way that broader social discourses and rhetorical practices of whiteliness are: representing predominantly white (and structurally whitely) institutional spaces and whites who function as their keepers as generous, kind, and hospitable in the democratic sense (all inclusive) while at the same time legitimating, enabling, and enforcing inequality in access and opportunity, linguistic supremacy, and discrimination within and beyond both the writing classroom and the writing centre. We argue that, as a field, we have known or have had the opportunity to know the truth of this hypocrisy for a very long time. What wonders us, then, is not why the scholars of colour and their accomplices whose work appears in this volume have produced essays in which rage and frustration are so often palpable, but why white and whitely writing centre folks would expect anything less of them.

Acclaimed Black Power activist and theologian Nathan Wright once wrote that "[i]n all fairness, black Americans cannot be asked to make emotional commitments to white friendships into which white people have historically built a guarantee of soon or late frustration." (1968, p. 117). In her poem, "For The White Person Who Wants to Know How to Be My Friend," Pat Parker wrote,

"The first thing you do is to forget that I'm black.
Second, you must never forget that I'm black."

In her book *Eloquent Rage*, Brittney Cooper writes that

Black women know what it means to love ourselves in a world that hates us. We know what it means to do a whole lot with very little, 'to make a dollar out of fifteen cents,' as it were. WE know what it means to snatch dignity from the jaws of power and come out standing. We know what it means to face horrific violence and trauma from both our communities and our nation-state and carry on anyway. But we also scream, and cry, and hurt, and mourn, and struggle. We get heartbroken, our feelings get stepped on, our dreams get crushed. We get angry, and we express that anger. We know what it means to feel invisible. (Cooper, 2018)

And with haunting resonance to Cooper's blast, in her keynote address to the IWCA, Neisha-Anne posed the question, "How the hell can this place be home if I am always alone?" (2018, p. 25).

We have had—we have all had—plenty of opportunity to know. And our field's collective (and ongoing) refusal to know—and to act on its knowledge—that racism and white supremacy persist and their persistence undermines any claim our field might make to inclusivity. We are not intersectional yet.

And so, we—Neisha-Anne and Frankie—wish to reframe the question of how white folks may be friends with People of Colour. Actually, we think that question is only important inasmuch as it draws the one who asks to the prior question—the real important question: how can I be a powerful and productive accomplice to People of Colour from within my field, from within my institution, from within my writing centre? And only when one can answer that prior question in the lived sense—by what one does and how and with whom—can the question of how to be a friend to People of Colour be addressed. We think this is what Dr. Vay actually meant when he said this is the right question to be asking: if we answer, "by being a good accomplice" and you listen and learn, then the question will have taken you to that "differential movement between possibilities of being" that constitutes prophetic love (Sandoval, p. 169).

And so it is with love that we offer to you our collective sense of what you, what we, as a field, must (a) let go of and (b) begin to do in order to be the accomplices that we have claimed we are.

DON'T TELL US TO WAIT ANYMORE!

Y'all think y'all know what patience is, but y'all don't really know.

Y'all think that

Patience is the capacity to accept or tolerate delay, trouble, or suffering without getting angry or upset

Y'all think that

Patience is the ability to endure difficult circumstances such as perseverance in the face of delay; tolerance of provocation without responding in annoyance/anger; or forbearance when under strain, especially when faced with longer-term difficulties.

Y'all think that

Patience is not the ability to wait, but the ability to keep a good attitude while waiting.

Let me tell you about patience. Patience is when

I am the only Black woman on the directors' level in the Office of Undergraduate Education.

Let me tell you about patience. Patience is

Me walking into my 1–1 meeting with my new supervisor and for the first time he asks if we can leave the door open cause he's trying a new open door policy. I say yes and sit down. He struggles for a min to say what's on his mind. I eventually say "Just say it." Had I known what was about to come out his mouth I would have told him to swallow that shit, but I was patient. He looks me full in my face and says "so—you're a Black woman right" and then proceeds to caution me against the stereotypes that plague women like me.

Patience is having the ability to hear that shit and not lose my shit.

Let me tell y'all something right quick—

Everybody knows that James Baldwin said, to be a Negro in this country and to be relatively conscious, is to be in a rage almost all the time right? Well look here, if you don't want me to be angry don't piss me off.

Let me tell you about patience. Patience is when

I am asked to speak up in the Vice Provost's directors' only meetings and *I* ask for patience as we, the academic support team, figure out our new roles since the last reorg. I say hey we've all got new roles in addition to the old responsibilities we've had, we're short staffed and working hard at filling those newly created positions and so I ask for your patience this semester, especially since none of y'all are qualified to do my job. I close with, please respect my expertise. The VP walks me back to the writing center and calmly shares that it is quite likely that the other directors all think that I am now talking about them. I shrug my shoulders, cause what she really want me to say in response to that. Look, I SAID WHAT I SAID. She asks if I don't care and I respond with "well, if any of them would come kick it with me every once in a while, they would know if I was talking bout them or not" To which she responds, well I don't think they visit the writing center cause they are probably scared of you.

Patience is hearing that shit and not losing my shit.

Let me tell you about patience. Patience is what

I have when the Black kids on campus flock to my office looking for a safe space.

Let me tell you about patience. Patience is

Ignoring your comments about my hair and not telling you about your own shit

Let me tell you about patience. Patience is

Being told that I do not look like a Writing Center Director and still going from an Assistant Director to Associate Director to Director of the Writing Center and now Director of Academic Support Services AND the Writing Center all in FOUR YEARS

Let me tell you about patience. Patience is

Saying the same shit and not being heard the same way every damn time.

Let me tell you about patience. Patience is

Me talking to you real plain right now instead of walking the hell up outta this field cause I said I wasn't talkin on this foolishness no more!

Let me tell you about patience. Patience is realizing that

I'm damned if I do, and I'm damned if I don't so guess what . . . I pick don't. Cause y'all don't listen and if you think I'mma waste my time preachin, languagin and laborin this morning then y'all got me all fucked up.

My name is Neisha-Anne S. Green and I am impatient, tired, and pissed da fuck off

I am quite shy by nature

As I think about what I need to write to you my chest is pounding and I am willing myself not to stop writing

I don't even know if I be making sense these days, but

I do know that I have to keep trying things til I get it right cause

I refuse to go crazy off the bullshit y'all do and say.

In Portland at Cs I gave y'all 4 reasons why I was pissed off and fired up

I said what I said then and what I said was

Your privilege means more to you than others' sufferation and re-education and I ain't performing for you no mo just so you could feel less guilty and more comfortable about your privilege

Reason number 2 is Y'all keep trying me . . . I wake up cursing the fact that your micro and macro aggressions have been tattooed on my soul and branded in my mind and I refuse to be dat one.

The 3rd why I have graduated from pissed off to fuck it is cause when it's your turn, you can't handle the pressure! Your fragility is real as fuck.

- I woke up on the day after the Presidential election of 2016 and carried on with my normal routine. I cussed morning as if it had somehow personified and made my way to work cussing the bad drivers of DC as they panicked at the sight of the roundabout that was there yesterday. As I walked into the library I could instantly feel a difference that was unlike any other difference. The library itself seemed to be mourning and its inhabitants, what little she housed that day, were in full-on mourning themselves. I walked by tear stained faces and heads hung way too low for long term comfort—quickly learning to avoid posing the normal "how you doing today?" greeting as I unlocked the writing center and began my work for the day. Not much had changed for me. I was still who I was, the world was still who it was turning on its regular axis with the same injustices occurring as before. I still looked like me and still expected to be treated the same way, not seen the same way and sometimes not heard just the same as any other day. In your absence, I carried about my day as I normally would have except for one small detail. While you were knitting pink pussy hats and deciding which safety pin to wear I made one change to my email signature and added three extra lines in a bold and sassy orange hue to make sure that it would be seen. These lines read:

- Allies are satisfied to quietly help and support.
- Accomplices support and help through word and deed.
- Accomplices actively demonstrate allyship.

The 4th reason why I have graduated from pissed off to fuck it is cause this really ain't my problem to fix, this be your burden to carry. I'mma do like Baldwin and give you your nigger back. "You're the nigger baby, it isn't me."

I also know that in these political games we play in the academy the games of having your token darkie, Hispanic, Asian, or Indigenous person in the department so you can say you're diverse

- the games of speaking up only at the end of faculty meetings cause that's when you're comfortable
- the game of continuing to ONLY teach the ever-fluid standard cause you can't bear to give up a lil piece of your privilege so that the others may finally be validated in what they bring from home
- the game of delaying my plea for help cause you don't want white people to panic

I have nothing left to lose that wasn't already
raped, stolen
or borrowed from me.

There is nothing that you can do to me that hasn't been done to me and, others who look like me who have

Rightfully earned a seat at Academia's table.

As the 2017 keynote in Chicago at the International Writing Center Association conference I called y'all out for your lack of diversity. I spoke directly to People of Color and asked us to get in this work and to stay in this work in spite of the trials and tribulations we face. I told People of Color to do away with the traditional view of double-consciousness and to learn instead to trust their own singular vision of themselves. I talked back to Paul Laurence Dunbar's We Wear the Mask and I told my People of Color that I had taken my mask off and destroyed it. I am myself all day everyday.

And lastly, since y'all are needy and kept asking what I would say to you I gave you this gift. I said:

I finally have the language and understanding to be able to try to explain what I've been feeling about the idea of allies, the lack of tangible and visible action with being an ally, and allyship in general. I purposely use the word *idea* to describe it all because I'm yet to see this fantasy that folk have created and professed became reality with any true substance or positive result.

Dr. Omi Osun Joni L. Jones gave us six rules for being what she called an *ally*; I share excerpts of five rules here. I find the word *ally* problematic, but not the rules, cause what I hear her really asking is for us to be accomplices. I wanted to make posters with Dr. Joni Jones's rules on them and plaster them everywhere.

Listen to what she says and tell me what you really hear:

Rule 1. "Allies know that it is not sufficient to be liberal. In fact the liberal position is actually a walk backwards. . . . We [must] move toward a radical rather than liberal position. . . . Allies must be willing to be warriors."

Rule 2. "Be loud and crazy so Black folks won't have to be! . . . This does not mean be reckless, strategizing is always important. . . . Speaking up does mean being able to relinquish some piece of privilege in order to create justice."

Rule 3. "Do not tell anyone in any oppressed group to be patient. Doing so is a sign of your privilege." Justice delayed is justice denied.

Rule 4. "Recognize the new racism, the new sexism, the old homophobia. It is institutional and structural."

Rule 5. "When called out about your racism, sexism, or homophobia, don't cower in embarrassment, don't cry and don't silently think that 'she's crazy' and vow never to interact with her again. . . . Be grateful that someone took the time to expose yours."

Tell me ya'll ain't hear her say take risks in each one of those rules. I see risks as being important to actually getting this work done. Minorities spend so much time checking ourselves to see if we're good enough to fit in and get in to do the work. I've long decided I was giving you back this problem of racism cause it isn't of my invention, or that of my foreparents, so since I'm giving you your problem back to fix, I've got a checklist for you—if you can't acknowledge the following then I got no time for you and you should keep out my way . . .

cause I'll know you're an accomplice when

1. you can acknowledge your privilege—confession is good for the soul . . . and the movement;

2. you can take a back seat and let the voices of the marginalized be heard loud and clear;

3. you have stopped expecting others to educate you on these issues—that's lazy and annoying.

4. you don't have to give yourself a title. Titles are overrated. If you have
   to say that you're against oppression, then chances are you're probably
   really not. If you have to announce that you're an accomplice, then I
   already don't trust you. All I really wanna see is that WERK.

   At Cs last year I grounded my argument for change by reminding you
   of Fannie Lou Hamer. I was out here LOUD TALKIN' like Auntie
   Fannie Lou—cause I'm out in these streets, SICK AND TIRED AH
   BEING SICK AND TIRED!!!

At the 2018 keynote in Auburn at IWAC, I said To define anti-racism
you have to understand how racism operates. Racism is about power, it
systematically disempowers People of Color. It systematically privileges
whites. It dehumanizes everyone. And racism accomplishes these things
by utilizing systems and institutions to advance its purposes. Anti-racism,
then, is active and determined resistance of structural and systemic racism in all its forms.

Then, yet again I called for the destruction of allies and the move
towards accomplices.

In 1963, in his book *Why We Can't Wait*, Dr. King said

"Some of the most vocal liberals believe they have a valid basis for
demanding that, in order to gain certain rights, the Negro ought to pay
for them out of the funds of patience and passivity which he has stored up
for so many years. What these people do not realize is that gradualism and
moderation are not the answer to the great moral indictment which, in
the Revolution of 1963, finally came to stand in the center of our national
stage. What they do not realize is that it is no more possible to be half free
than it is to be half alive." (2000)

In the same sense (King says), "the well-meaning or the ill-meaning
American who asks: 'What more will the Negro want?' or 'When will
he be satisfied?' or 'What will it take to make these demonstrations
cease?' is asking the Negro to purchase something that already belongs
to him by every concept of law, justice, and our Judeo-Christian heritage. Moreover, he is asking the Negro to accept half the loaf and to
pay for that half by waiting willingly for the other half to be distributed
in crumbs over a hard and protracted winter of injustice. I would like
to ask those people who seek to apportion to us the rights they have
always enjoyed whether they believe the framers of the Declaration of
Independence intended that liberty should be divided into installments
doled out on a deferred-payment plan. Did not nature create birth as a
single process? Is not freedom the negation of servitude? Does not one
have to end totally for the other to begin?" (2000)

AND

"It is because the Negro knows that no person—as well as no nation—can truly exist half slave and half free that he has embroidered upon his banners the significant word NOW." (2000)

Let me tell you about patience. Patience is

Me talking to you real plain right now instead of walking the hell up outta here cause I said last yr that I wasn't talkin on this foolishness no more!

Listen! And learn the political history of the writing center: a history that has been told and re-told for decades.

MIC DROP.

REFERENCES

American University Working Group on the Influence of Slavery (2018). "Influence of Slavery on American University: Initial Findings and Recommendations: A Report to Members of the Community." American University: https://www.american.edu/president/diversity/upload/FINAL-Slavery-Working-Group-overview.pdf.

Grand Scholar Wizard. (2019). Post to WPA-L. 22 March.

Howard, R. M. (2004). Deriving backwriting from writing back. *The Writing Center Journal, 24*(2).

Inoue, A. (2019, March 14). "*How Do We Language so People Stop Killing Each Other, or, What Do We Do About White Language Supremacy?*" [Chair's Address]. Conference on College Composition and Communication. David L. Lawrence Convention Center, Pittsburgh, PA, United States.

King, M.L. (2000). *Why We Can't Wait.* Signet.

Smith, A. L. (1969). *Rhetoric of Black Revolution.* Allyn and Bacon, Inc.

Villanueva, V. (2006). Blind: Talking about the new racism. *The Writing Center Journal, 26*(1).

Wright, N. (1968). The crisis which bred black power in the black power revolt. (F. B. Barbour, Ed.). Porter Sargent.

INDEX

ABOUT THE AUTHORS

EDITORS

Frankie Condon is an Associate Professor in the Department of English Language and Literature at the University of Waterloo. Her books include *I Hope I Join the Band: Narrative, Affiliation, and Antiracist Rhetoric; Performing Anti-Racist Pedagogy in Rhetoric, Writing and Communication*, co-edited with Vershawn Ashanti Young; and *The Everyday Writing Center: A Community of Practice*, co-authored with Michele Eodice, Elizabeth Boquet, Anne Ellen Geller and Margaret Carroll. She is a member of the APTLY OUTSPOKEN! Collective, a group of academics and activists committed to speaking and writing against anti-Black racism, settler colonialism, and, indeed, all forms of racism in the USA and Canada. Frankie has been the recipient of the Federation of Students Excellence in Undergraduate Teaching Award (OUSA) and the Outstanding Performance Award (for excellence in teaching and scholarship) from the University of Waterloo.

Dr. Wonderful Faison (Dr. Wonderful) is an assistant professor and chair of the English & Foreign Languages department at Langston University. Her research heavily focuses on race, racism, and Black language use in academic spaces, i.e., the writing center. Her articles, "Black language, black bodies: Exploring the use of black language in the writing center," and "Race, retention, language, and literacy: The hidden curriculum of the writing center," help push the boundaries and limitations of pedagogical and theoretical responses to race and racism.

AUTHORS

Dianna Baldwin has been involved with writing center work since she was a graduate student at Middle Tennessee State University. After earning her PhD in English with a focus in composition and rhetoric, she became the associate director of The Writing Center @ Michigan State University for ten years where she found her passion for being an advocate for students' voices. She is currently the Writing Center Director at Longwood University, where she works with undergraduate students and mentors them in becoming professionals in their chosen career paths.

Nicole I. Caswell (she/her/hers) is an Associate Professor of English and Director of the University Writing Center at East Carolina University. Her research interests include writing centers, writing assessment, and emotional labor/work. Nicole's research has been published in the *Journal of Writing Assessment, Journal of Response to Writing, Composition Forum*, and various book chapters. Her book *The Working Lives of New Writing Center Directors* (coauthored with Grutsch McKinney and Jackson) was awarded the 2017 International Writing Center Association Book of the Year.

Mitzi Ceballos is an MA student and teaching assistant in the English department at the University of Washington, where she teaches first year composition. Her work focuses on rhetorics of immigration and anti-racist pedagogy and assessment. She has a BA in English from Boise State University, where she worked in the writing center for four years. She currently serves as the main editor of *Confluences: a Washington State Anthology of Student Work*, and as discussion facilitator for the composition department's anti-racism reading book club.

Romeo García is Assistant Professor of Writing and Rhetoric Studies at the University of Utah. His research on local histories of settler colonialism, settler archives, decolonial critique, and Mexican Americans in South Texas appears in *The Writing Center Journal, Community Literacy Journal, constellations, Rhetoric Society Quarterly,* and *College Composition and Communication.* García is co-editor (with Damián Baca) of *Rhetorics Elsewhere and Otherwise,* winner of the 2020 Conference on College Composition & Communication Outstanding Book Award (Edited Collection). Garcia's current interests include the decolonial research paradigm's impact on composition and rhetorical studies; archival research; the cultural imaginary of border(ed)landers of South Texas; and, community building in and outside of academia.

Neisha-Anne S. Green is Faculty Fellow for the Frederick Douglass Distinguished Program and Director of Academic Student Support Services and the Writing Center at American University in Washington, DC. She teaches in the American University Experience program, created by AU faculty, staff and students to ensure that diversity, inclusion, free speech and freedom of expression are part of the core curriculum. Neisha-Anne is a multidialectal orator and author proud of her roots in Barbados and Yonkers, NY. Always interrogating and exploring the use of language as a resource, she is an ally who is getting better at speaking up for herself and others. Neisha-Anne continues to collaborate and publish on anti-racism and anti-racist pedagogy and is working on her book, *Songs From A Caged Bird.*

Douglas S. Kern is a Professor of English at Valencia College in Florida. His cross-disciplinary research focuses on representations of murder, killing, and death in the revolutionary drama of Amiri Baraka and language plurality within intercultural communication and composition. He currently serves as an Academic Advisor for Gale's *Contemporary Literary Criticism* and *Drama Criticism* series, while his more recent publications can be found in the forthcoming book, *New Perspectives in Edward Albee Studies (Volume #4—Edward Albee: Influence), Continuum: The Journal of African Diaspora Drama, Theatre and Performance,* and *Praxis: A Writing Center Journal.*

Talisha Haltiwanger Morrison (she/her/hers) is Assistant Professor of Writing and Director of the OU Writing Center and the Expository Writing Center at the University of Oklahoma. Her research interests and areas include writing center administration and community engagement, applying Black feminist and critical race theory to her administrative and engagement work. Her recent research explores the cross-campus experiences of Black student-tutors on historically white university campuses and how tutor perspectives can inform writing center practice.

Dr. Bernice Olivas teaches writing and rhetoric at Salt Lake City Community College. She is a First-Generation, Indigenous Mexican American scholar who began her academic career as a high school dropout with a G.E.D. In 2007, Bernice joined the McNair Scholars Program. In 2010, she completed her B.A. in English from Boise State University with a creative writing emphasis and continued on to complete her MA (2012) in the teaching of English and her PhD (2016) in Composition and Rhetoric at the University of Nebraska–Lincoln.

Moira Ozias is Assistant Professor of Higher Education at Grand Valley State University. She worked for over fifteen years in writing center administration where she was continually challenged as a white woman to unlearn dominating educational practices and learn critical praxis toward racial justice. Her current research grows out of these experiences and examines the ways that white supremacy shapes the inner lives and dominating practices of white women, including herself, in higher education.

Jill Reglin is a professor in the Integrated English department at Lansing Community College (Lansing, Michigan) where she also serves as Lead Faculty in the Learning Commons Writing Studio. Reglin has taught community college composition since 1996 both at LCC and Mott Community College in Flint, Michigan. She is from Milford, Michigan, and earned her degrees from Alma College and Michigan State University.

Trixie G. Smith is Director of The Writing Center and Red Cedar Writing Project at Michigan State University, and faculty in Writing, Rhetoric & American Cultures and the Center for Gender in Global Contexts. Recent publications include the collection *Graduate Writing Across the Discipline: Identifying, Teaching, and Supporting*; articles in *Feminist Pedagogies, WAC Partnerships Among Secondary and Post-Secondary Institutions*, and *Composing Feminist Interventions*, with upcoming articles on reimagining doctoral writing through cultural rhetorics and embodiment in the writing center. Her motto is that we're all just humans learning with/from other humans (you know, with bodies, feelings, lives outside the academy).

Anna K. Treviño is pursuing a PhD in Composition, Rhetoric, and Literacy at the University of Oklahoma and is Graduate Student Assistant Director at the OU Writing Center. Her primary research interest is the intersection of the politics of education and identity, and focuses on the dynamic relationships between the writing and literacy experiences of marginalized students and space (writing centers, first-year composition, and the First-Year Experience). She is committed to developing more just ways of teaching and interacting across communities, and she grounds her work in Xicana feminism and counter-storytelling as a Critical Race Methodology.